W9-ANH-294

THE INTIMATE

garden

THE INTIMATE garden

BRIAN D. COLEMAN

PHOTOGRAPHS BY WILLIAM WRIGHT

Gibbs Smith, Publisher
TO ENRICH AND INSPIRE HUMANKIND
Salt Lake City | Charleston | Santa Fe | Santa Barbara

First Edition
12 11 10 09 08   5 4 3 2 1

Text © 2008 Brian D. Coleman
Photographs © 2008 William Wright except
          pages 58–69 © 2008 Huntley Hedworth

Published by
Gibbs Smith, Publisher
P.O. Box 667
Layton, Utah 84041

Orders: 1.800.835.4993
www.gibbs-smith.com

Designed by m:GraphicDesign / Maralee Oleson
Printed and bound in Hong Kong

Library of Congress Cataloging-in-Publication Data
Coleman, Brian D.
  The intimate garden / Brian D. Coleman ; photographs by William Wright.—
1st ed.
      p. cm.
  ISBN-13: 978-1-58685-856-8
  ISBN-10: 1-58685-856-4
  1. Urban gardens. I. Title.

SB473.C6425 2008
712'.6091732—dc22
                          2007038388

CONTENTS

ACKNOWLEDGMENTS

The author and photographer both wish to thank all of the homeowners and gardeners across the country who opened their gardens to us for this project. Our favorite editors, Madge and Lisa, have once again helped us produce a beautiful book and we extend to them our warmest gratitude. Bill wishes to thank his patient wife, Pauline, and daughter, Ella, and Brian thanks Sandy for his support—after all, it's those around us who help us fulfill our potential.

FACING: The house beckons at dusk as its lights glow with rich colors echoed in the garden. *(Seattle)*

INTRODUCTION

Intimate gardens are special places, somewhere to relax, forget one's troubles, and nurture the senses and soul. Whether it's a formal parterre of classically clipped boxwood or a secret hideaway tucked behind an ornate wrought-iron gate, a garden can come in many shapes and forms. It all began with a colorful curbside garden in Seattle, a mélange of expertly blended annuals and perennials that was designed to complement the fall palette of an early-twentieth-century home.

After photographing the garden with talented photographer Bill Wright, it wasn't long before both of our curiosities were piqued and we began searching for other interesting examples of gardens around the country, all with one thing in common—each was a creative, individual and intimate retreat.

Our search took us to the wildflower-covered hills of Mill Valley, California, where we found an oasis nestled on a mountainside knoll. Hidden behind plantings of coast live oak and mature rhododendrons, the garden has been lovingly tended by the same owner for more than thirty years. Filled with swaths of purple and pink rhododendrons and azaleas set beneath a canopy of white and pink flowering dogwood and delicate Japanese maple, the garden is divided into rooms connected by slate paths winding through swaths of primordial ferns. And what makes this garden so unique are the breathtaking views from every angle of nearby San Francisco and the mountain meadows surrounding the house, which are peppered with wildflowers each spring.

Another special garden just south of San Francisco represents the lifetime passion of a dedicated couple who rescued a derelict but historic Japanese tea house garden. Built in 1897 by a wealthy American who was enamored with Japanese culture, it was centered on a traditional Japanese teahouse overlooking a koi-filled lagoon. Each plant and stone was carefully thought out, symbolic of man's relationship with nature. This is reflected in the garden's name: "Higurashi-en: A Garden Worthy of a Day's Contemplation." Now returned to its original beauty, the garden has been placed on the National Register of Historic Places and is listed by the Smithsonian Institute as the "most authentic privately owned Japanese garden" in the country.

No garden book would be complete without elegant southern examples, and so we have included three. The first is in historic Savannah, Georgia, a city with a long horticultural legacy—when the city was originally laid out in 1793, it was designed around a series of lushly planted town garden squares. Private, small "secret" gardens are found throughout the city, and we visited one whose owner has patiently restored it to its original nineteenth-century elegance. The garden is divided into a trio of rooms—at the entrance is the sunken court centered on an antique cast-iron Fiske fountain, followed by the compass garden, so-called for its circular mound of native holly clipped into the four points of a topiary compass, and the sitting garden in the rear sheltered underneath the spreading branches of several mature deciduous trees.

Charleston, South Carolina, is known for its classical architecture and gardens. One of its grand homes was built in 1799 overlooking the Charleston Harbor, and a decade ago, abandoned and in disrepair, was rescued and restored, its gardens redesigned by well-known Charleston landscape architect Sheila Wertimer. Reflective of the stately home's origins, the garden was divided into a series of connecting parterres meant to be viewed from above on the wide piazzas that run along the side of the

house: a formal garden with a brick reflecting pond and classic square of common box, a more colorful and informal clipping garden filled with beds of fragrant pink sweetheart roses, and a back garden shaded by handsome trees including a graciously spreading two-hundred-year-old southern magnolia.

A few blocks away, the Calhoun Mansion is one of Charleston's most elaborate residences. Built in 1876, the 24,000-square-foot home had its gardens restored several years ago by Sheila Wertimer to a classic elegance befitting the Italianate mansion. A series of intimate garden rooms, each centered on a water feature or sculpture, was designed to wind around the house, with classic symmetry and plantings such as borders and balls of tightly clipped Japanese boxwood tying the garden together.

Not all gardens need be grand or formal, however. Take, for example, the Portland, Oregon, garden of a local horticulturist who is enamored with the Orient. Set on a pair of small inner-city lots are a magical collection of smiling stone Buddhas, sandstone fragments from ancient Indian temples, and bamboo wind chimes. Native plants such as twice-bearing raspberries and rhododendrons are combined with exotic *Canna 'Musifolia'*, hardy banana, and trailing abutilon to create an intimate and mystical retreat.

Exotic gardens can be found in many climates, such as the stunning, brightly colored example we discovered in sunny Pasadena. Set around a storybook 1926 Spanish Colonial Revival home, the garden is filled with exotic succulents, such as a fifteen-foot-tall *Euphorbia candelabrum,* and accented with splashes of color, including a blood red Crown of Thorns. In the rear an unused guest house was converted into the owner's writing studio and surrounded with a tropical paradise of bright blue and orange bird-of-paradise, orchids, and a Technicolor red, orange and pink bougainvillea.

England is known for its tradition of fine gardening, and we traveled to the heart of the British Isles to find an example. Located in Nottingham on the edge of Sherwood Forest, this urban garden is set behind a tidy Edwardian villa. Its owners have meticulously transformed the former concrete block breezeway into an enchanting and manicured miniature Eden. The garden was divided into terraces on two separate levels with salvaged brick, and the entire yard was surrounded by a curving brick wall of stone from a demolished church and a folly was added at the rear. Beds were filled with annual color as well as the lush greenery of hostas for perennial form and foliage.

Gardening on a steep hillside is never easy, but the ingenuity of a Seattle landscape designer shows how a problematic hill can be transformed into an inviting and unified space. Hidden from prying eyes on the street level above, the garden is like a secret paradise tucked below. With the house as the center, a series of private yet connecting garden rooms was created around it, each accented with a different architectural feature, such as a bubbling fountain, a classic stone statue, or planted urns on pedestals. To unify the steep elevations of the site as well as provide soil stability, curving brick and stone terraces were built and outlined with dwarf box.

And for those who live in urban centers, conservatories can become that special garden retreat. We were fortunate to photograph an elegant example on Manhattan's Upper East Side, the rooftop conservatory constructed by the addition of another floor during the recent restoration of a single-family five-story brownstone. Stunning nineteenth-century stained glass panels in the signs of the Zodiac were used as windows, while a Tiffany bas-relief marble wall fountain became the focal point of the room. Hanging baskets of colorful orchids and goldfish plants and ornate majolica planters of palms, blushing philodendrons, and rex begonia made the conservatory a lush and elegant respite from the bustling city.

We hope that these eleven beautiful gardens, each a unique and special creation, will be inspiration for others to create intimate gardens of their own, magical retreats to replenish and rejuvenate their souls and senses.

FACING: Spring blossoms of *Agapanthus africanus* 'Peter Pan' surround a gurgling stone fountain. *(Seattle)*

ALL-SEASONS HILLSIDE
IN SEATTLE

Gardening on a hillside is never easy. Drainage, soil erosion, access to planting areas and just plain maintenance are common obstacles. Robyn Cannon, whose home was built in 1907 on the steep northwestern slope of Seattle's Queen Anne Hill, knows this only too well. The simple shingled bungalow purchased by her husband, Don, in 1964 boasted sweeping views of Elliott Bay but was perched on a very precipitous hillside.

For twenty years Robyn and Don have worked on restoring the home's interiors with the help of her father, John Roehm, a retired master carpenter. But challenged by the narrow, steep lot, which was hard to maintain, the couple landscaped it simply with a loose, cottage-style garden that had little interest except in the height of summer. In the winter of 1998, a serious sewer line break in the hillside following an unusual Seattle snowstorm changed the lackluster garden forever. Fixing the problem necessitated digging up all of the existing vegetation and rerouting the entire hill's drainage. The project took more than a year to complete, but rather than becoming discouraged, Robyn decided to make the most of the situation. So she planned out an entirely new garden for the muddy hillside, linking and formalizing all the levels of the property into a cohesive design.

Work began with the garden's "hardscape"—that is, permanent features such as brick walls and walkways, stonework, wrought-iron fences, fountains and architectural ornamentation that form the backbone of the garden. Carefully planning the placement of these elements helped to establish pathways and focal points so that foundation plantings could be arranged to their best advantage around the elements. Robyn wanted to ensure that the garden had interest throughout the seasons and looked as good from inside the house as it did from the outside. So she stood in every window and examined each view carefully before she began, placing architectural focal points to be seen from both inside and out.

In her attempt to unify the steep elevations of the site, Robyn created a series of sweeping, serpentine brick and stone terraces that

FACING: Serpentine brick retaining walls create a series of terraces up the steeply sloping lot; 'Sally Holmes' roses bloom throughout the summer.

curve around the house and are outlined by more than 2,200 dwarf boxwoods forming tight hedges. The terraces also provide important stability to counteract soil movement and erosion on a slope deemed highly sensitive by the City of Seattle.

Inspired by French gardens of white roses and agapanthus, Robyn planted a bed of thirty creamy white 'Sally Holmes' roses on the hill above the house in a sunny terrace outside her kitchen window. Bordered by towering agapanthus 'Blue Giant' and velvet green true dwarf boxwood, the massive hillside of roses provides a dramatic shared garden view for Robyn as well as her fortunate uphill neighbors.

Except for those few neighbors, the garden is hidden from prying eyes on the street level above. Descending into it is like entering a secret paradise tucked into the center of the bustling city. Fifty steep steps (made from concrete streetcar pilings) lead down through the secluded shade garden, which is centered on a towering, seventy-five-year-old cedar. Robyn used a variety of hydrangea, hosta, ivy and thickets of her favorite ferns (lady fern, ostrich fern, Japanese painted fern, autumn fern) to create a peaceful woodland glen. A brick pathway leads from the bottom of the street steps to the main level of the garden. With the bungalow as the center, Robyn created a series of private yet connected garden rooms around the house. Each area is accented with a different architectural feature, such as a bubbling fountain,

a classic stone statue, or planted urns on pedestals.

Every inch of space was put to use. A charming eight-foot-wide rose topiary and herb allée was carved out along the western side of the house, which was formerly just an ivy-covered hillside. Twenty-foot-tall Italian cypresses and more dwarf boxwoods frame the rose and herb beds and provide protection from the wind. A gurgling fountain bordered by tuberoses and agapanthus provides the garden focus and helps drown out the sound of traffic from the street below.

The north side of the slope, terraced since the turn of the century with huge pieces of granite ship ballast and overgrown with ivy and big leaf maples, required the most extensive drainage work after the storm. Since neighboring houses rely on the stability of the hillside, the site was excavated to ten feet below grade and then regraded with crushed gravel. An engineered retaining wall of interlocking "Pisa" stone created the terraces, which were camouflaged with yew hedges and hydrangeas planted in three levels. Colors were alternated between purple 'Oregon Pride', tiny cerise 'Preziosa' and hot pink 'Glowing Embers' for more visual interest. A compact herringbone brick patio was developed below the retaining wall for dining, accented by large planted stone urns and a small fountain. And for added privacy, a tight hedge line of Leyland cypress fronted by dark green English yew was planted to

ROBYN'S CANONS OF EUROPEAN-STYLE GARDEN DESIGN

Here are six principles of classic garden design Robyn shares with her clients:

1. Adopt the European principle of using every inch of space and living in it to the fullest.
2. Courtyard gardens emphasize privacy, so create a series of hedged garden rooms to unify and define your space.
3. Building a garden without structure is like writing a sentence without punctuation. Remember that good-quality hardscape provides a backbone upon which you can layer plants.
4. Choose ornamentation carefully. It's better to use a few large architectural elements in a tight space than too many small decorative items to create visual impact.
5. Appreciate foliage over flowers. It will help your garden appear lush throughout the seasons.
6. Choose your favorite flowers and plant them en masse for greater effect.

screen an unattractive adjacent apartment building.

Two levels of straight-grain fir decks open off the southern side of the house and extend the living area into the garden. Adjacent to the lower deck, a tiny lost space was reclaimed by creating an intertwining boxwood knot garden accented by hot pink fuchsia 'Firecracker' in the centers. Anchored by a classical statue of Nike of Samothrace, this small secret garden is a pleasant surprise when gazing down from the decks above.

After Robyn had created her garden, her friends began asking her to help them with their own, so she began her own business, Classic Courtyards LLC. The design and installation company specializes in small European-style urban gardens. Robyn's story is proof that it really is sometimes possible to turn a sow's ear into a silk purse.

RIGHT: Rows of cypress and dwarf boxwood create a narrow allée along the western side of the house. An antique rooster from France is an amusing accent.

FACING: A classic statue of Nike presides over a tiny knot garden of dwarf boxwood and hot pink fuchsia 'Firecracker' on the lower level.

ABOVE: Yellow *Hemerocallis* 'Stella de Oro' daylily is a favorite perennial.

RIGHT: Lady fern is a favorite in the shade garden.

ABOVE: Two levels of decks were added to the bungalow to expand the living space into the garden and take advantage of the sweeping westerly views.

RIGHT: Swaths of color are created by the white 'Sally Holmes' roses, delicate pink *Hydrangea macrophylla* 'Glowing Embers' and yellow *Hemerocallis* 'Stella de Oro' daylilies.

FACING: The warm colors of bright red delphinium 'Red Caroline' are paired with a lemon yellow canna and pink *Hydrangea macrophylla* 'Glowing Embers' near the front entrance walkway.

FACING: Formal brick paths and curving retaining walls add structure and form to the garden. Dwarf boxwood hedges line the beds that are planted with banks of hydrangeas, ferns, and seasonal color.

RIGHT, TOP: Daylily in a delicate purple and cream combination lends spring and early summer color.

RIGHT, BOTTOM: A bloom of *Agapanthus africanus* 'Peter Pan' is ready to burst with an intricate lavender display.

ABOVE, LEFT: Summer is heralded by brilliant yellow *Coreopsis tinctoria* (golden tickseed) around the north allée's fountain, while silver cascades of lavender provide a pleasing contrast.
ABOVE, RIGHT: Spring blossoms of *Agapanthus africanus* 'Peter Pan' surround a gurgling stone fountain.
FACING: All-seasons hillside garden plan.

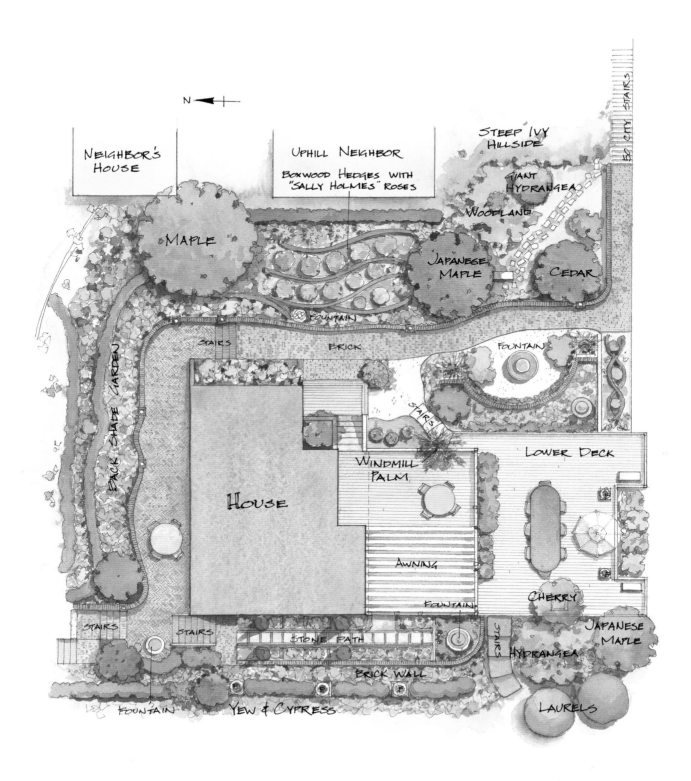

NEIGHBOR'S HOUSE

UPHILL NEIGHBOR

BOXWOOD HEDGES WITH "SALLY HOLMES" ROSES

STEEP IVY HILLSIDE

50 CITY STAIRS

GIANT HYDRANGEA

WOODLAND

MAPLE

JAPANESE MAPLE

CEDAR

FOUNTAIN

BRICK

FOUNTAIN

STAIRS

BACK SHADE GARDEN

STAIRS

HOUSE

WINDMILL PALM

LOWER DECK

AWNING

FOUNTAIN

CHERRY

JAPANESE MAPLE

STAIRS

STAIRS

STONE PATH

HYDRANGEA

BRICK WALL

FOUNTAIN

YEW & CYPRESS

LAURELS

MOUNTAINTOP GARDEN
IN MILL VALLEY

When Glenn Haldan and his wife, Virginia, were looking for a home with some room for a garden over thirty years ago, they had nearly given up hope. They had been living with their two small children in scenic Mill Valley, California, and wanted to stay in the area. It was an easy commute across the Golden Gate Bridge to Glenn's job in San Francisco, the schools were excellent, and they enjoyed the area's scenery and small-town atmosphere.

But houses were hard to find and their patience had worn thin when their realtor showed them one last prospect. A long driveway led up to the 1937 Tudor, perched on the side of Mount Tamalpais. On an acre of grounds, the setting was spectacular, with sweeping mountain vistas giving way to views of the bay below and the sparkling San Francisco skyline in the distance. Glenn and Virginia knew immediately this was the house of their dreams.

The house was secluded on a knoll, nestled behind a grove of live oak and mature plantings of rhododendrons and azaleas. The garden, however, had had little attention or maintenance for the past several decades. A large pine tree along the driveway obscured the sunlight, and Glenn was soon informed that its roots were invading the neighbor's foundation. A hedge of vigorous *Pittosporum tenuifolium* had been allowed to grow to over fifteen feet on the south side of

the property, screening out not only the residents on the hillside below but also scenes of sailboats dotting the crystal blue waters of San Francisco Bay. And a large area next to the house that was intended to become a patio instead was an unfinished mud pit (much to the delight of the children).

So Glenn set out to redefine the garden, opening it up to the bright California sunlight and the dramatic views while preserving its private and sequestered setting. With the help of his gardener, Casper R. Curto of Casper Landscape Design (Curto has now worked in the garden for the past two decades), garden rooms were laid out and structure was created. The long, winding asphalt and gravel driveway was repaved with more pleasing cobblestones. Retaining walls

FACING: The two-tiered koi pond is surrounded by colorful Japanese maple (*Acer palamatum* 'Crimson Queen'), grape hyacinth (*Muscari armeniacum*), azaleas and ferns.

of Colorado stone were added, and the scalloped leaves and delicate violet-blue blossoms of shade-loving Kenilworth ivy, also known as ivy-leafed toadflax (*Cymbalaria muralis*), was encouraged to creep out from the crevices. The overpowering pine was removed, revealing beautiful mountain vistas.

Next to the house, the mud pit was filled in, with some difficulty due to the steep site (a special ramp from the road below allowed a tractor to bring in several tons of fill dirt and stone). A terraced pool was added between the patio and the guest-house on the lower east slope of the property and surrounded with pots of roses and a table of bonsai that prosper in the sunny setting. Sheltered by a small grove of white birch and sweetly scented gardenia trees, another small patio was carved out of the steep slope along the back of the house on the west and filled with pots of orchids and succulents, including the waxy-leaved echeveria (Hen and chickens) and ornamental Queen Victoria's agave (*Agave victoriae-reginae*). A greenhouse was added on the lower slope to rotate the ever-growing collection of orchids (now numbering over two hundred; vandas, cattleyas, oncidiums and odontoglossums are among the favorites). And to greet visitors, a softly gurgling waterfall and koi pond were installed near the front steps (migrating blue herons also appreciate the pond's gold-finned inhabitants, however, so netting must be used to protect the fish).

Meandering slate paths were built to wind around the steep slopes of the hillside and connect the rooms of the garden. From the front steps, an allée was created across the north garden through the curving and twisted branches of majestic Coast live oaks (*Quercus agrifolia*). Swaths of rich color—deeply hued purple and pink rhododendrons ('Purple Splendor', 'Pink Pearl', 'Noyo Chief') and lipstick red azaleas ('Ward's Ruby', 'Pride of Dorking')—were planted. They were bordered by the lush fronds of primordial ferns—Tasmanian tree ferns (*Dicksonia antarctica*),

antler-like staghorns (*Platycerium bifurcatum*) and the slightly woody asparagus (*Asparagus densiflorus* 'Meyers')—that line the path to the slate-roofed guest cottage. Japanese maple (*Acer palmatum*) and white and pink flowering dogwood (*Cornus* 'Eddie's White Wonder', *Cornus florida* 'Cherokee Chief' and 'Cloud Nine' among the most spectacular) were planted between the live oak for color and more canopy.

The multilevel pool terrace was defined with stately obelisks and wooden Italian columns lining its perimeter in classical symmetry. Paved with Montana stone, the terrace holds pots of pink, lavender and creamy white roses, including the sweetly

FACING: Colorful slate paths wind around the north slope past an ancient, twisted cypress, pink and white flowering dogwood and bright red Japanese maple.
ABOVE: A stone Buddha head serenely smiles at visitors on the moss-covered front steps.
RIGHT: Slate paths meander beneath a canopy of coast live oak in the north garden.

fragrant, blush pink 'Cecile Brunner' (sweetheart rose), the creamy yellow hybrid tea Graceland and the deep reddish pink Eva Gabor hybrid tea. (Eva, an accomplished rose horticulturist, liked to counsel that roses, like men, need constant attention.) More pots were clustered about the pool for displays of seasonal color: brightly blooming cyclamen during the winter, followed by tulips each spring and then red, white and pink impatiens (*Impatiens wallerana*) during the summer and fall.

Sculptures and artwork were placed throughout the pool garden—a carved stone head on the front steps, a curious bronze giraffe peeking into the pool terrace, antique life-size cast-iron roosters guarding the patio. And tying it all together are the breathtaking vistas from every corner of the garden: San Francisco Bay, Alcatraz and the downtown San Francisco skyline to the south; to the west, mountain meadows that are peppered with pink and purple wildflowers each spring; and above it all,

the craggy peak of Mount Tamalpais rising majestically to the north.

Another path was laid along the south side of the house leading from the pool terrace through azalea and scented hibiscus to the back patio garden. A secluded sitting area was set up underneath the shady branches of a *Magnolia soulangia* 'Jane' and a nearby twelve-foot-tall persimmon tree and was soon an intimate spot for morning coffee and afternoon lemonade; it is also a favorite rest stop for the resident squirrels who are treated to snacks of the honey-sweet persimmons each fall.

As with all good gardens, the work is never done—bromeliads are being hung in the rhododendrons lining the driveway, pots of tulips are being planned for next spring, and Glenn is trying to think of new ways to outsmart the crafty blue herons. But both Glenn and Virginia find time each day to reflect on their good fortune in finding this special mountaintop garden and the beauty it has brought into their lives. ✿

ABOVE, LEFT: A moss-covered wooden bench is a tranquil spot to reflect beneath lilacs, asparagus ferns and Japanese maple in the shady north garden.
LEFT: An aboriginal stone head rests peacefully amongst lush asparagus ferns.
FACING: A multilevel stone terrace and pool open off the house on the east and are accented with architectural salvage and pots of perennial and seasonal color. Sweeping views of the bay and San Francisco are to the south.

FACING: Stately wooden columns stand above the slate-roofed guest cottage and demarcate the eastern patio border and pool.
ABOVE, LEFT: A crusty wrought-iron gate is given new life as a decorative screen to hold pots of succulents on the back terrace.
ABOVE, RIGHT: Delicate red blossoms cluster on an *Asparagus densiflorus* fern in a weathered wrought-iron planter next to the pool.

LEFT: Spikes of bright purple Pride of Madeira (*Echium fastuosum*) wildflowers pepper the steep mountain slopes during springtime.
ABOVE: A mischievous elf peeks out beneath pots of roses, azaleas and impatiens, which provide displays of seasonal color on the upper pool terrace.
FACING: Thick clouds of morning mist slowly evaporate off the surrounding hillsides at sunrise.

ABOVE: Pots of waxy-leaved Hen and chickens (echeveria) are clustered on the back terrace.
RIGHT: Lush ferns, including Tasmanian tree ferns (*Dicksonia antartica*) and staghorns (*Platycerium bifurcatum*), line the steep driveway.
FACING: Mountaintop garden plan.

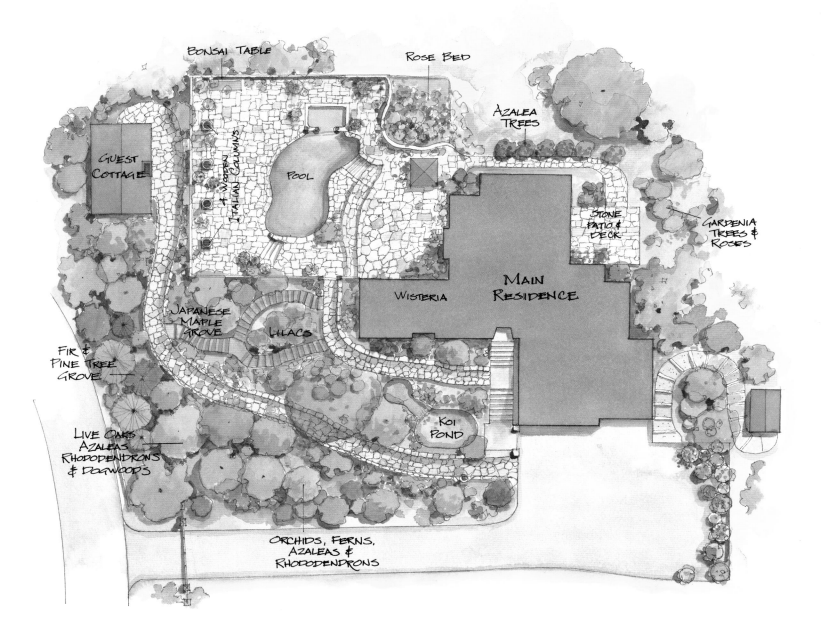

BONSAI TABLE

ROSE BED

AZALEA
TREES

GUEST
COTTAGE

4 WOODEN
ITALIAN COLUMNS

POOL

STONE
PATIO &
DECK

GARDENIA
TREES &
ROSES

JAPANESE
MAPLE
GROVE

LILACS

WISTERIA

MAIN
RESIDENCE

FIR &
PINE TREE
GROVE

KOI
POND

LIVE OAKS
AZALEAS
RHODODENDRONS
& DOGWOODS

ORCHIDS, FERNS,
AZALEAS &
RHODODENDRONS

SECRET GARDEN
IN SAVANNAH

Gardens are a cornerstone of Savannah, Georgia. The original city plan, designed and laid out by James Oglethorpe in 1733, was arranged around a series of six garden town squares, each lushly landscaped with majestic live oaks dripping with Spanish moss, swaths of brightly colored spring-blooming azaleas, historic monuments and fountains. Over the next 125 years, the number of squares grew to twenty-four, and despite the Revolution, Civil War, several epidemics, an earthquake

and more than a few hurricanes, Savannah somehow managed to always survive, surrounded and constantly renewed by the verdant beauty of its magnificent gardens.

The legacy of urban gardens in Savannah was continued in the nineteenth century as neighborhoods of brick town homes were laid out on narrow lots just 100 by 60 feet wide. Each lot contained a two-to-four-story brick home, a carriage house with horse and buggy stalls and servants' quarters above (and a "necessary house" in back); most families had a cow, a goat, chickens, dogs and even a small vegetable garden. As the economy began to recover from the Civil War by the late 1870s, ordinances were passed relegating the animals to the city outskirts. "Urban pleasure gardens" began replacing the dusty animal yards. Hidden behind tall brick walls, these secret gardens could only be seen in tantalizing glimpses from the street through decorative wrought-iron gates.

When Jim Morton purchased his 1856 home in Savannah's Historic District in 1973, little remained of its former "pleasure garden." The house had been divided into four apartments and the narrow lot's forlorn side yard was filled with debris. Standing on the balcony of the carriage house at the back of the lot, Jim methodically planned the garden's restoration. Referencing photos in the Georgia Historical Society archives, he realized that most of Savannah's early gardens were influenced by their owners' travels and "grand tours" of England, France and Italy. And so he decided on his own plan, one that was classically inspired but by

FACING: The compass garden is centered on a compass topiary created from clipped native holly (*Ilex vomitoria*). The surrounding parterre is outlined with Japanese boxwood (*Buxus microphylla* var. *japonica*) and planted with annuals and perennials.

necessity sized to fit into the narrow 30-by-80-foot yard between the original brick garden walls and the house.

A trio of garden rooms was conceived with plantings and focal points scaled to the space. The elegant sunken court was created to greet visitors as they enter through the garden's original wrought-iron gate. Old bricks in traditional "Savannah gray" were used for the terraced walls, and Tennessee slate on the paths. Jim made the lucky find of a derelict yet rare cast-iron, two-tiered Fiske fountain from the 1870s in a neighboring garden. The fountain was placed at the center of the sunken court and surrounded by parterres edged with clipped Korean boxwood (*Buxus microphylla* var. *koreana*) for classic symmetry. The four corners of the court were demarcated by statues of stone putti playing musical instruments. White Indian hawthorn (*Raphiolepis* sp.) and sword fern (*Nephrolepis exalta*) were placed within the boxwood

ABOVE, LEFT: The delights of the garden can be glimpsed through the gate.
ABOVE, RIGHT: The original wrought-iron gate beckons visitors into the garden; stepping over the white marble threshold signifies entrance into Paradise.
FACING : The garden opens into the sunken courtyard, which is outlined in Korean boxwood (*Buxus microphylla* var. *koreana*) and centered on an antique fountain. The terraced side beds are planted with rows of double white H. H. Hume azaleas and Savannah holly (*Ilex* x *attenuata* 'Savannah'). The original carriage house and slave quarters are at the back.

circles, while rows of double white H. H. Hume azaleas and Savannah holly (*Ilex x attenuata* 'Savannah') were used to line the terraced beds. Large clumps of green striped bamboo (*Arundinaria*) were planted along the western wall of the garden and have now grown to forty feet, providing an effective screen from the neighboring house. Honoring an old Southern tradition, a white marble threshold was placed at the garden's entrance: the act of stepping over white marble symbolizes one's entrance into Paradise. And a round millstone from Jim's great-grandfather's farm was laid in the stone just beyond the gate to emphasize the family's agricultural heritage.

1990s. The compass topiary is outlined with Japanese boxwood (*Buxus microphylla* var. *japonica*) and planted with seasonal perennials—purple spider flower (*Cleome spinosa*), butterfly weed (*Ascelpias tuberosa*) and blazing star (*Liatris spicata*). Perennials, Jim points out, are often used as annuals in the semi-tropical climate of Savannah. More garden sculptures were used as focal points, including a marble sculpture of a horse's head that Jim carved himself during art school forty-five years ago and a seventeenth-century terra-cotta Italian olive oil storage urn embossed with the Medici coat of arms, which regally presides over the back of the garden.

From the sunken court, one enters the compass garden—the second of the three rooms—by stepping up two steps and passing underneath a wrought-iron arch dripping with tangles of sweetly fragrant Confederate jasmine (*Trachelospermum jasminoides*). A pair of cast-stone Spanish urns cloaked in English ivy (*Hedera helix*) rest on either side of the arch and help demarcate the entrance, while two twenty-five-foot-tall crape myrtle trees (*Lagerstroemia indica*) provide bright splashes of pink summer color. The compass garden is centered on a circular mound of clipped native holly (*Ilex vomitoria*) accented with the letters of the four points of the compass shaped in topiary. The unusual design was suggested by Jim's friend Louisa Farrand Wood, niece of Beatrix Farrand (the well-known garden designer). Louisa, an ardent gardener in her own right, helped rekindle the restoration of many Savannah gardens during the 1980s and

Stands of bonsai are strategically placed within the surrounding beds of hardy purple and pink azaleas, 'Formosa' and 'Pride of Mobile' among the favorites. Many of the bonsai are decades old, products of patient care and pruning by bonsai artist and grower Luigi Trapaini.

The last of the three garden rooms is a comfortable sitting garden nestled between the rear of the home and the carriage house. Sheltered underneath the spreading branches of several mature deciduous trees—Chinese weeping cherry, live oak and Chinese tallow—the sitting garden is a shady retreat out of view of the street and main garden. A nineteenth-century French limestone wall fountain helps drown out street noise and adds to the secluded and private atmosphere.

Inviting and romantic, this secret space is once again a garden of pleasure in this city of beautiful gardens. ❦

FACING: Leaves collect at the rim of the Fiske fountain.

ABOVE, LEFT: A terra-cotta Grecian urn rests at the base of the fountain, which is surrounded by sword fern (*Nephrolepis exalta*).

ABOVE, RIGHT: A stone putto is hidden among the English ivy (*Hedera helix*) at one corner of the sunken court room.

LEFT: Horned masks glower on the sides of cast-stone urns, which guard the entrance to the compass garden.

ABOVE: An imposing seventeenth-century terra-cotta Italian storage urn presides over the rear of the garden.

FACING: Purple spider flower (*Cleome spinosa*) and butterfly weed (*Ascelpias tuberosa*) are planted among the Japanese boxwood for displays of spring and summer color.

ABOVE: Stands of patiently pruned bonsai, many of which are decades old, rest among lushly blooming 'Pride of Mobile' azaleas.
FACING, LEFT: Spanish moss (*Tillandsia usneoides*), an epiphytic bromeliad, happily hangs in strands from the oak trees.
FACING, RIGHT: The original carriage house and slave quarters at the rear of the garden are now used for garden storage; here, bales of pine straw are ready to mulch and line the beds.

THE SPANISH MOSS STORY

Spanish moss (*Tillandsia usneoides*) is really not a moss at all but rather a flowering member of the bromeliad family. An epiphyte, it has no roots and hangs in tree branches throughout the southeastern United States, as it favors warm, humid climates. Spanish moss gets nutrients from rain and air and propagates by small fragments blown by the wind or carried by birds for their nests. It can grow so thick that it blocks the sunlight and slows down its host tree's growth. Harvested commercially for more than two centuries, many tons were shipped to Detroit for automobile seats, and it was in demand for mattresses, as it was said to make the coolest stuffing. Chairs advertised as stuffed with "horsehair" were, in reality, often just stuffed with Spanish moss (it was much cheaper). And during Prohibition, Spanish moss was even turned into gin in Louisiana and Florida. If you use it in your home, be sure to treat it for bugs beforehand—microwaving or boiling in water both work well—as it often contains chiggers.

ABOVE: A nineteenth-century French limestone wall fountain provides a pleasing focal point for the rear sitting garden.
ABOVE, RIGHT: Creeping fig vine (*Ficus pumila*) clambers over the brick walls.
RIGHT: A classic marble horse head, carved by the homeowner during his training at art school, is proudly displayed in the compass garden.
FACING: Secret garden plan.

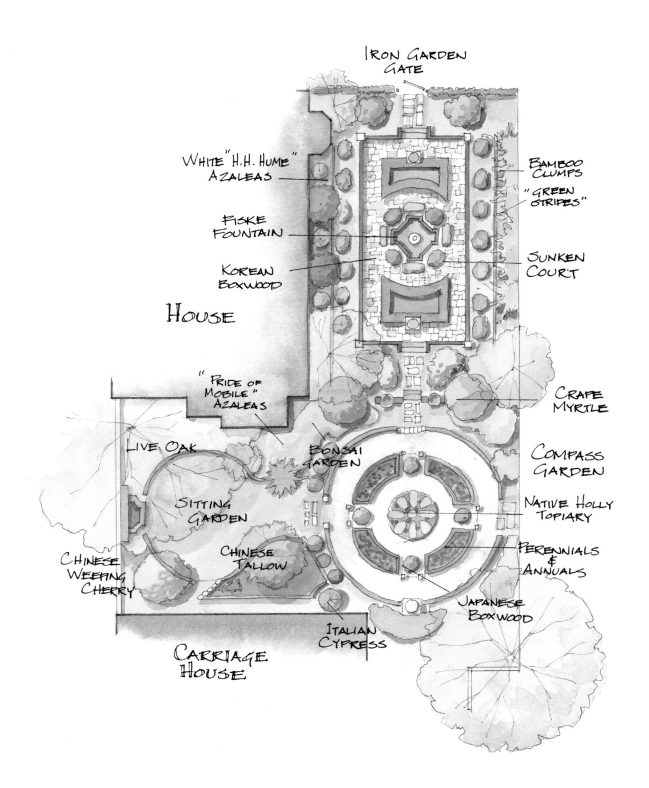

Iron Garden Gate

White "H.H. Hume" Azaleas

Bamboo Clumps

"Green Stripes"

Fiske Fountain

Korean Boxwood

Sunken Court

House

"Pride of Mobile" Azaleas

Crape Myrtle

Compass Garden

Live Oak

Bonsai Garden

Native Holly Topiary

Sitting Garden

Perennials & Annuals

Chinese Weeping Cherry

Chinese Tallow

Japanese Boxwood

Italian Cypress

Carriage House

AESTHETIC CONSERVATORY
IN MANHATTAN

When the owners of this five-story brownstone on New York's Upper East Side purchased it in 1998, they hired architect and designer David Parker and interiors historian and preservationist Mimi Findlay to help in its restoration. Over the next several years, the building was meticulously restored to a single-family residence, its original 1882 Aesthetic movement grandeur returned with ornate wallpapers, period lighting and museum-quality furnishings.

As a crowning touch, a conservatory was placed on the top by the addition of a sixth floor. Since the exterior of the building was landmarked, special care was required to meet New York City Landmarks Commission requirements. For example, to maintain the visual integrity of the original building, the addition could not be visible from the street. A six-foot setback was thus designed, which necessitated a complex structural system to support the new floor and conservatory. Additionally, the owners decided to clad the north exterior wall of the conservatory in copper in order to set it apart from the masonry structure below. Construction was complicated, as the house was already occupied and materials had to be hand-carried through the English basement and then hoisted up the back. A crane was used to set the roof in place.

A rare set of brilliantly colored English Aesthetic movement stained glass windows in the signs of the zodiac was acquired at auction and incorporated in the walls of the room. Eleven windows were purchased, and the missing one—Virgo—was re-created by talented artisans. A stunning Tiffany bas-relief marble wall fountain, featuring cavorting dolphins and a grotesque mask spouting a jet of water into a basin, was installed on the east wall; crowned with an overhead arch of a strutting peacock in gold mosaic tile, the fountain became the focal point of the room. Parker designed an intricate marble mosaic floor of sparkling gilt glass rosettes with cartouches and scrolls of soft green, white and gold Jerusalem limestone. The whole design was outlined in midnight blue lapis to coordinate with the stained glass windows. A glass

FACING: The sixth-floor conservatory sparkles with a Tiffany marble wall fountain, antique stained glass windows, a mosaic tile floor and hanging baskets of 'Golden Showers' orchids and goldfish plants.

LEFT: Delicately carved dolphins cavort in front of a mask spouting a stream of water from the Tiffany marble fountain.
ABOVE, RIGHT: A delicate spray of *Oncidium* 'Golden Showers' orchids hangs in front of the Tiffany fountain.
FACING: Surrounded by Australian tree ferns, rex begonia, ivy leaf geraniums and orchids, the marble wall fountain is attributed to L. C. Tiffany.

and steel arched and beamed roof was constructed in England by Machin Conservatories. Woodwork was fabricated to match that in the rest of the home. Walls were given a faux Jerusalem limestone treatment to echo the color of the mosaic floor tiles.

The owners are enamored with orchids, and thus the arching beams overhead were hung with wire baskets of delicately branching sprays of tiny gold- and yellow-flowered *Oncidium* 'Golden Shower' orchids and the shiny, bushy leaves and puckered orange blossoms of goldfish plant (*Nematanthus wettsteinii*). Fanciful nineteenth-century Majolica jardinières decorated with symbols of nature—water lilies, cherry blossoms, sparrows, butterflies and hummingbirds—were filled with palms. The slow-growing staple parlor palm, or Neanthe bella (*Chamaedorea elegans*), and the fan-shaped Chinese fan palm (*Livistona chinensis*) sit alongside the apple-green, swordlike fronds of bird's nest ferns (*Asplenium nidus*) and the boat-shaped, shiny foliage of blushing philodendron (*Philodendron erubescens*).

A pair of tiered wire planters custom made in England were placed on either side of the fountain to hold more plants— Wooly tree ferns (*Dicksonia antarctica*), silver and pink rex begonia (*Begonia* 'New York Swirl') and, of course, more orchids. Pots of bright red ivy leaf geraniums (*Pelargonium peltatum*) were added for color. The small heart-shaped leaves of an enthusiastic creeping fig vine (*Ficus pumila*) were trained to creep up the wall, while the perforated fronds of a Swiss cheese plant (*Monstera deliciosa*) were let float in the basin below for an exotic touch.

An important Reform Gothic oak sideboard by Daniel Pabst was set along the west wall as a counterpoint to the wall fountain, its shelves displaying more Aesthetic period ceramics.

Filled with light throughout the day, the conservatory has become a favorite retreat for the owners, a spot to enjoy a moment of relaxation away from the hustle and bustle of the busy city beyond the stained glass doors. 🌸

FACING: Tiered wire planters made in England rest on either side of the fountain and are planted with Australian tree ferns, swirling rex begonia and brightly colored ivy leaf geraniums below.
ABOVE: Peacocks, a favorite symbol of the Aesthetic period, crown an arch at the top of the fountain in hand-cut gold mosaic tiles.

LEFT: The colors of the late-nineteenth-century stained glass zodiac windows are echoed in the mosaic tile floor. The Victorian-style wire furniture was made in England by Rayment Wireworks.
ABOVE: Stylized sunflowers surround the zodiac signs in a typical Aesthetic design.
FACING, LEFT: The intricate mosaic tile floors feature rosettes of gilt glass along with designs in deep blue lapis, suggesting the opulence of a Turkish palace.
FACING, RIGHT: The stained glass windows glow at night from the roof outside.

ABOVE, LEFT: An important oak sideboard by Daniel Pabst in the Reform Gothic style holds a collection of Minton ceramic pots and vases. A rare 1881 Minton majolica garden seat in the "Passion Flower" pattern holds a hardy cream and green dieffenbachia (dumb cane) in a cobalt blue Minton jardinière.

ABOVE, RIGHT: A large Minton jardinière with stylized hummingbirds and bamboo is planted with Chinese fan palm, blushing philodendron and bird's nest fern.

FACING: Aesthetic conservatory garden plan.

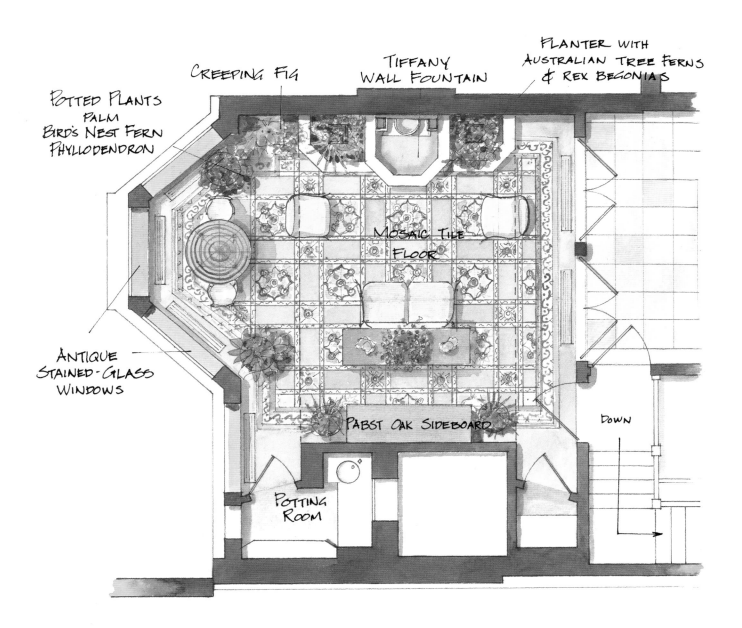

POTTED PLANTS
PALM
BIRD'S NEST FERN
PHYLLODENDRON

CREEPING FIG

TIFFANY
WALL FOUNTAIN

PLANTER WITH
AUSTRALIAN TREE FERNS
& REX BEGONIAS

ANTIQUE
STAINED-GLASS
WINDOWS

MOSAIC TILE
FLOOR

PABST OAK SIDEBOARD

DOWN

POTTING
ROOM

EDWARDIAN
TOWN GARDEN
IN ENGLAND

England is known for its tradition of fine gardening. Meticulously maintained gardens can be found throughout the country, many just small urban plots but still cared for with as much passion and pride as larger estates. One such garden is located in Nottingham, which is in the East Midlands, the center of the country. Set on the edge of Sherwood Forest, home to the colorful legends of Robin Hood, Nottingham has an ancient past.

Distinguished Victorian and Edwardian villas still line the city's leafy boulevards, including Elm House, a semidetached villa built in 1903. A handsome structure when originally constructed, it had been the family home for the prosperous local butcher and was outfitted with the finest detailing available at the time. Decorative stained glass was set into the front door and landing windows; elegant trim in a lighter Edwardian taste was used throughout the home; and in the rear, an intimate courtyard was included, with just enough room for a small lawn and planting beds, perhaps even a tiny kitchen garden.

But by the time Malcom Bescoby and Michael Blood saw the house listed for sale in 1978, the once grand villa had fallen into hard times: the house was uninhabitable and stank with rubbish. The walls were painted a depressing industrial green. The yard was filled with garbage and overgrown with two-foot-high weeds and grass. But the home still

had a classic Edwardian appeal that was hard to resist. It was structurally sound, without damp or dry rot, and the original Art Nouveau stained glass was still intact. The back opened onto a pleasant terrace with potential. So Malcolm and Michael decided to rescue the forlorn structure.

They began by removing more than eighty bags of debris from the house and yard. Lace-covered French glass doors were installed across the rear to bring inside much-needed light and views of the garden. An awkward and oversized kitchen that formerly occupied the entire back of the house was converted into a more pleasing spacious dining room whose tiny windows were replaced with a colonnade

FACING: The small garden is divided into a pair of terraced rooms on two levels. In the foreground, the lower terrace is filled with pots of hostas and brightly colored annual geraniums and begonias.

of floor-to-ceiling arched windows to give a better view to the terrace.

After restoring the interior spaces, the pair next turned their attention to the garden, which in the rear consisted of a six-foot-tall wall of concrete breezeblocks with a lone castor plant languishing in the middle of the weeds. The unsightly concrete walls surrounded the entire yard and presented a significant design challenge. Salvaged bricks were found to replace the concrete, and a more interesting curved profile was created, broken up by occasional small windows and niches and accented with a stone-capped lintel on top. The 35-by-75-foot yard was then divided into terraces on two levels, helping to define and separate the space into two connected, yet individual, garden rooms.

A brick-lined lower patio was laid directly off the back of the house, providing a pleasant area for reading the morning newspaper on the Gothic wrought-iron bench. Its walls were purposefully kept low (five feet) to ensure the space remained open and inviting, as the neighbor's garden is an important part of the view. An upper terrace, raised up three and a half feet (six steps), was added by shaping the formerly rectangular area into pleasing curves of clipped green lawn centered on a Gothic stone font. Vines were trained on the brick walls to help soften and reduce their heaviness—classic English ivy (*Hedera helix* 'Gold Heart'), its glossy, heart-shaped leaves brightened with a splash of creamy yellow in their centers; silvervein creeper (*Parthenocissus henryana*) with rich, bluish green leaves streaked with silver that turn bronze and crimson red in the autumn; and showy crimson glory vine (*Vitis coignetiae*), which gives a spectacular display of scarlet leaves each fall. For spring and early summer color, the rich purple-violet blossoms of clematis 'Vyvyan Pennell' were trained to clamber up a trellis and cascade happily back down into the yard.

To visually expand the small garden, a decorative wrought-iron gate was added in the west wall, its open grillwork giving tantalizing glimpses of the neighbor's adjoining greenery (which Michael and Malcolm also plant and maintain).

Architectural elements were used throughout to lend historic atmosphere. An eight-foot-tall Haddstone column topped by a lichen-covered globe now presides majestically over the shady northwest corner of the garden in classical elegance, while salvaged putti and urns peek out from niches and rest on top of the brick walls.

A pair of life-sized, nineteenth-century terra-cotta greyhounds guard the lower terrace. A large lot of reclaimed brick from an old farmhouse was used along with stone from a demolished church in Derby to build a folly at the northeast corner of the yard. Antique tiles, terra-cotta urns and Victorian wrought-iron window grilles were incorporated in its design for more interest. The ceiling was covered with glass for protection against the elements, and it quickly became one of the favorite spots in the garden, used nearly every month of the year for a spot of afternoon tea or a candlelit evening supper.

The stone font was encircled with the lush greenery of potted common box (*Buxus sempervirens*) alternating with the densely packed rosettes of Queen Victoria's agave (*Agave victoriae-reginae*), which glow with their golden leaf borders. Four Japanese maples (*Acer palmatum*)—reddish purple 'Bloodgood', dwarf 'Crimson Queen', golden 'Aureum' and refreshing lemon-yellow and orange 'Orange Dream' were added. Along with golden honey locust (*Gleditsia triacanthos*) and the coarse-textured leaves of northern catalpa (*Catalpa speciosa*), the plants form a rich backdrop for the seasonal plantings of colorful begonias and geraniums.

Heart-shaped hostas abound both in beds and pots for perennial form and foliage: glossy golden green *Hosta nigrescens* 'Sum and Substance'; tall, wavy hosta hybrid cultivar

'August Moon', with its lavender flower spikes in late summer; dreamy hosta hybrid cultivar 'Wide Brim', with big blue-green leaves with creamy yellow edges; and large *Hosta sieboldiana* 'Big Daddy', with heavily textured, intense blue-green leaves. The bright green fronds of the Australian tree fern (*Alsophila australis*) along with a feathery Phoenix palm *Phoenix roebelenii* (Pygmy Date Palm) on the edge of the upper terrace were used to demarcate the two levels with their lacy, exotic foliage.

The last major project, recently completed, was the addition of a hexagonal pond and fountain constructed with sections of reclaimed carved sandstone removed from a local Victorian mansion. Designed to be viewed from the kitchen, the gurgling pool was stocked with koi and carp and quickly became a favorite neighborhood stop for frogs, dragonflies and birds.

Michael admits that he has been so successful in his garden design that several neighbors, after peering over the fence, have commissioned him for their own terraces, providing him with a small second career in his retirement. The time-honored English tradition of a well-kept garden is still going strong in Nottingham.

FACING: An antique wrought-iron gate opens into the neighboring garden. Clematis 'Vyvyan Pennell' cascades over the brick wall, while a Japanese maple (*Acer palmatum* 'Crimson Queen') provides a lush background for seasonal plantings.
ABOVE: A moss-covered statue of a Grecian maiden peers delicately from beneath a canopy of holly-leafed barberry (*Mahonia aquifolium*) and Japanese mock orange (*Pittosporum tobira*) along the north wall.

FACING: A folly was built in the rear corner of the garden using reclaimed brick and stone and salvaged architectural artifacts. The room was covered with an inconspicuous glass ceiling, making it comfortable for year-round use.

LEFT, TOP: Antique tiles, carved stone and terra-cotta fragments give the folly a whimsical and colorful appeal.

LEFT, BOTTOM: Potted geraniums in a row rest happily on a brick shelf. The distressed character of the reclaimed bricks was carefully preserved, adding to the folly's age and charm.

RIGHT: An irregular profile and several small windows covered with antique wrought-iron screens make the brick garden wall more interesting.

HEAVENLY HOSTAS

While hostas are thought to have originated in coastal China and Korea, it was Japan that popularized their use, where they have been prized for centuries for their lovely blue-green coloring and lush foliage. Brought to the West in the mid-nineteenth-century, hostas soon became popular perennials, easy to grow in nearly all climates (hardy in zones 3–8). Hostas continue to be developed (there are now over 2,500 varieties) and have a wide range of leaf textures and forms as well as colors, ranging from chartreuse to deep green to sunny yellow. The following are general tips for their care:

1. Light is important. While hostas do best in bright shade, there are also sun-tolerant cultivars—usually with more yellow and gold coloring—that do well if given adequate moisture. Hostas do not grow well in deep shade.
2. Add organic material to the soil when planting: leaf mold, peat moss, well-rotted compost. Soil requirements are straightforward, and hostas perform well in any rich, organic soil with a pH of 6.5 to 7.5.
3. Water regularly, at least an inch per week. Drooping leaves or burnt tips indicate insufficient water.
4. Pests, especially slugs and snails, can quickly damage a hosta, so use slug bait or other controls (beer in a shallow container works well), especially in the spring when new growth begins.

The American Hosta Society (www.hosta.org) is a good resource for more information.

ABOVE: A concrete doe nestles quietly beneath the leaves of hosta 'El Dorado' in a shady corner.
FACING: The garden is visually extended with a gate opening into the neighboring yard at its west end. An antique stone font is encircled with potted common box alternating with Queen Victoria's agave. 'Maverick Pink' geraniums provide a splash of summer color.

LEFT: An elegant eight-foot-tall Haddstone stone column crowned with a globe presides over the northwest corner of the garden.
ABOVE: A classic terra-cotta bust merrily purviews the garden from his hidden niche high in the English ivy–covered brick wall.
FACING: An octagonal pool constructed of salvaged Victorian sandstone fragments can be viewed from the kitchen windows. An Australian tree fern helps demarcate the upper level terrace.

LEFT: A Gothic wrought-iron bench is the perfect spot for morning coffee on the lower terrace. The soft chartreuse leaves of northern catalpa, lemon-yellow Japanese maple 'Orange Dream' and sunny hosta 'Gold Standard' (*Hosta fortunei*) add an enchanting golden glow.

ABOVE: Handsome woodwork and the original stained glass in the front door were part of the Edwardian villa's appeal that convinced the owners to save it.

FACING: Edwardian town garden plan.

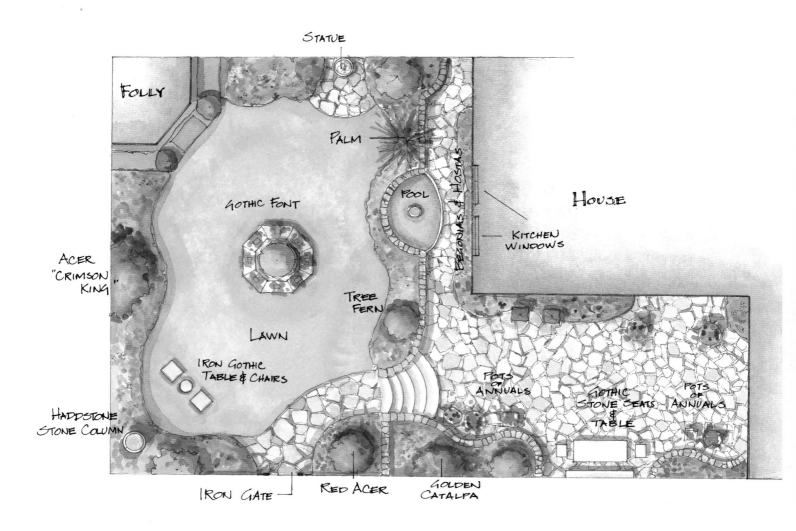

STATUE

FOLLY

PALM

ACER "CRIMSON KING"

GOTHIC FONT

POOL

BEGONIAS & HOSTAS

HOUSE

KITCHEN WINDOWS

TREE FERN

LAWN

IRON GOTHIC TABLE & CHAIRS

HADDSTONE STONE COLUMN

POTS OF ANNUALS

GOTHIC STONE SEATS & TABLE

POTS OF ANNUALS

IRON GATE

RED ACER

GOLDEN CATALPA

SUCCULENT GARDEN
IN PASADENA

When Michael Llewellyn and his partner Tom Rotella first saw the 1926 Spanish Colonial Revival bungalow for sale in Pasadena, they were attracted to not only the house but also its unusual and beautiful gardens. The front entrance, flanked by a pair of spiny, six-foot-tall agaves, beckoned with a slightly disconcerting, otherworldly charm. More exotic succulents could be glimpsed beyond, such as the neck-craning *Euphorbia candelabrum,* whose fifteen-foot arms towered over the red-tile roof.

Splashes of color, including a blood red Crown of Thorns (*Euphorbia milii*) and a seven-foot-tall, hot orange Lion's Paw (*Leonotis leonurus*) beneath a spreading Chinese elm, added to the exotic appeal.

It was not a surprise to discover that this house and its gardens were anything but ordinary. The house was originally built in Brentwood as a secret gift from silent screen star Tom Mix to his mistress Dorothy Sebastian, a George White's Scandals showgirl who became a movie actress and later married another cowboy film legend, William Boyd (aka Hopalong Cassidy). During her heyday, Dorothy entertained costars such as Joan Crawford and Anita Page here. But by 1987, the once-charming bungalow faced demolition, unwanted and outdated. Fortunately, its owners recognized its provenance and decided instead to donate it to Cal State, which dismantled and stored it until 1991, when artists

Michael and Rennie Rau Marquez purchased the historic home and moved it to its present site, a sunny lot on a palm-lined boulevard in Pasadena.

The Marquezes spent more than a year meticulously restoring the house, returning the elaborately stenciled living room and coffered dining room ceilings to their original splendor and replacing modern, reproduction chandeliers and wall sconces with period-appropriate pieces. The original fireplace with stenciling and handsome Malibu tiles was cleaned and put back into working order. The stucco exterior was painted a pleasing golden peach, and interior rooms were given new life in a bright Mexican

FACING: The front walkway is bordered with an exotic mix of colorful succulents and drought-tolerant plantings: ice plant, Lion's Paw, Kangaroo Paw, cereus and red Crown of Thorns. A spreading Chinese elm provides shade on the west side of the yard.

LEFT: A romantic stuccoed archway leads from the shady side yard into the front garden.

ABOVE: A delicate fortnight lily blooms in front of a prickly pear cactus pad in a pleasing contrast of textures.

FACING: A fat barrel cactus nestles amongst the spiny stems of gray-green agave in the front yard.

palette of primary blues, yellows and oranges inspired by Frida Kahlo's Casa Azul in Mexico City. The Marquezes designed and planted the cactus and succulent gardens around the home and were awarded a Pasadena Golden Arrow Design Award in 1993 for their outstanding work.

Luckily, when Michael and Thomas bought the home in 2004, only minor cosmetic work was needed. They refined the gardens by adding focal points of statuary, graveling dirt paths that turned to mud during the winter rains, and putting out pots of seasonal color. Raised planting beds in the rear were removed, and a new vista was created down the center of the yard through an arched trellis.

The gardens were designed to be drought-tolerant, given their southern California location, so rooms of cacti and succu-lents were created. The front walk sets the desert tone with the enormous agave sentinels, which lead to a delightfully chaotic front yard mélange of towering *Euphorbia*, stately cereus and low succulents, colorful fortnight lilies, bird-of-paradise (*Strelitzia reginae*), lantana (*Lantana camara*)—so-called "ham and eggs" for its yellow and pink blooms—and graceful fountain grass (*Pennisetum setaceum*). Fragrant yellow Angel's Trumpet (*Brugmansia*) and the sprawling Chinese elm provide a partial canopy during the hot California summers.

Profusely blooming oleander clambers over the top of a story-book archway on the east side of the house. A weathered wooden gate opens to the shady east side yard, which is planted with sweet-smelling gardenias, cheerful dahlias and an enormous and profusely blooming magenta-purple bougainvillea.

The rear gardens were divided into three rooms. A flagstone patio was created against the back of the house—a pleasant retreat to sit in comfortable Adirondack chairs and contemplate an adjacent small pond and fountain planted with horsetails and bordered by lantana and rosemary. A cacti and succulent garden dominated by a twelve-foot-tall 'Monstrous' "Montrose Totem Pole" (*Lophocereus schottii*) was created on the west side of the yard and bordered with needled prickly pear (*Opuntia*), cowhorn (*Euphorbia grandicornis*), shiny smooth aloe and gnarly *Myrtillocactus*. A sunny grove of nine citrus trees sited at the back of the garden provides fruit throughout the summer and fall.

Michael converted an unused guest house—the Casita—into his writing studio and surrounded it with a subtropical room of electric blue-and-orange bird-of-paradise (*Strelitzia reginae*), giant bird-of-paradise (*Strelitzia nicolai*), a primordial fern tree (*Dicksonia antarctica*), calla lilies (*Zantedeschia aethiopica*), clivia (*Clivia miniata*), orchids (*Cymbidium*) and a Technicolor red, orange and pink bougainvillea, which swarms over the red tile of the studio. Pots of geraniums and kalanchoe add even more color on the porch of the Casita. Several mature trees, including a spreading jacaranda (*Jacaranda mimosifolia*), a crepe myrtle (*Lagerstroemia*) and a thorny floss-silk tree (*Chorisia speciosa*) provide overhead shade. A central path encircles the pond, winding past an arched trellis covered with potato vine and banked with rose bushes, and leads the eye through the backyard rooms with tantalizing glimpses into this secret paradise. ❧

FACING: Intensely red Crown of Thorns overflows onto a ceramic Mexican statue on the front porch patio.
LEFT: Kalanchoe, *Echeveria*, cabbage and ivy all happily share a basket on a wire table on the west side patio.
BELOW: Burro's tail trails from a Talavera planter on a sunny garage wall in the rear garden.

CACTI TIPS

Of course, even cacti need maintenance. The key is vigilance, Michael explains. Here are some other tips:

1. Inspect the plants weekly and remove dirt, dust and cobwebs that quickly accumulate in the spines.

2. If a plant is too leggy, don't be afraid to prune it back. A good pair of quality leather gloves is a must, plus a healthy respect for those spines at all times.

For beginners as well as more experienced gardeners, Michael highly recommends Miles Anderson's *World Encyclopedia of Cacti and Succulents*.

The cactus room in the rear garden bristles with prickly pear in the foreground, euphorbia on the top left and *Lophocereus schottii* right rear.

ABOVE: An agave leaf shelters the sharp spikes of a barrel cactus in the front garden.

LEFT: Architectural fragments in a corner of the rear garden include ironwork and a sphinx from the owner's former residence in New Orleans. The *Amor* placard is by California artist Carlo Marchiori.

LEFT: Steps to the Casita, a small guest house/study in the backyard, are lined with pots of colorful geraniums, kalanchoe and cacti. Multicolored bougainvillea climbs up the porch railings onto the walls.

ABOVE: *Lophocereus schottii* can be glimpsed through the iron grillwork in the east side yard garden gate.

FACING: The colorful side porch opens onto a brick patio that is crowded with groups of cacti in pots. Wisps of potted lavender phlox provide a delicate accent.

ABOVE: Tangerine and lime trees shade a secret bougainvillea nook in the rear garden.

RIGHT: A curving path divides the rear garden rooms, with the cactus and succulent room on the right, the citrus grove at the rear and a subtropical room on the left shaded by a fig tree canopy.

FACING: Succulent garden plan.

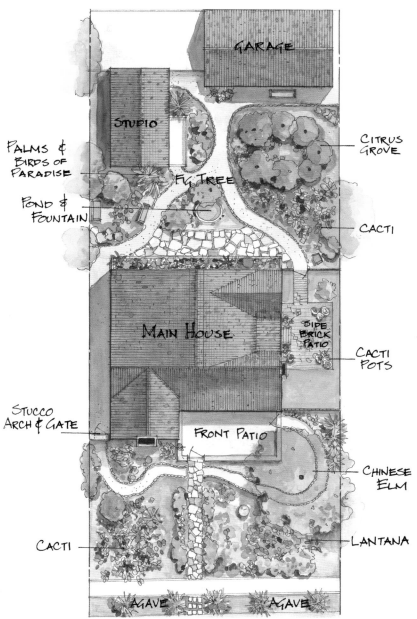

GARAGE

STUDIO

PALMS &
BIRDS OF
PARADISE

FIG TREE

CITRUS
GROVE

POND &
FOUNTAIN

CACTI

MAIN HOUSE

SIDE
BRICK
PATIO

CACTI
POTS

STUCCO
ARCH & GATE

FRONT PATIO

CHINESE
ELM

CACTI

LANTANA

AGAVE

AGAVE

CLASSIC ELEGANCE
IN CHARLESTON

Charleston, South Carolina, is known for its historic homes and gardens, many built in the eighteenth and early nineteenth century, when the influence of Robert Adam was at its height. Adam, a Scottish architect, was well liked in the United States, where his proportionate and symmetric classicism was considered a good alternative to the Georgian architecture of the early British colonists.

So, in 1799 when Caspar Christian Schutt, a wealthy shipping merchant, purchased a long, deep lot on East Bay Street overlooking the Charleston Harbor, he built his home in the newly fashionable Adam (or Federal) style. Though each floor was just one room wide and contained only two rooms, the rooms were nonetheless large—twenty-four feet square—with many elegant details: graceful mantels, ornate plaster moldings and, in the center foyer, a grand elliptical staircase that swept up three stories.

In the 1830s new owners bought the lot next door and razed the home that was on it, giving them sufficient space to add large piazzas, or porches, on the south side of their house. (A typical Charleston feature, the wide piazzas take advantage of fresh air and sea breezes, which are greatly appreciated during the humid and hot southern summers). And room was also created for a long side garden.

In the twentieth century, the house passed through several hands, and by 1990 it had been vacant for eight years: there were pigeons nesting inside, collapsing ceilings and plants growing in the walls. Then, fortunately, Wayland H. Cato Jr. decided to rescue the derelict but historic structure and return it to its former elegance. Sadly, no original garden remained, so the Catos contacted local Charleston landscape architect Sheila Wertimer, who performed magic, transforming the formerly nondescript grounds into three classically inspired garden rooms reflective of the historic style of the home.

The first room is the formal garden, entered through the street vestibule and handsome wrought-iron gates. Opening off the marble-block-paved first-floor piazza, the

FACING: A classic parterre of four quadrants outlined by common box is centered on a terra-cotta pot planted with 'Crimson Queen' Japanese maple in the formal garden.

LEFT: The pond, seen from the second-floor piazza, is stocked with carp and planted with classic zebra grass, ancient Egyptian papyrus and water lilies.

ABOVE: Four lofty Washingtonian palms stand on each corner of the brick pond in the formal garden. A privet hedge of Japanese ligustrum backed by a border of ironwood trees provides shade and privacy.

FACING: East of the pond, a small terrace was created against the brick wall. A hedge of Japanese yew softens the wall, and four crape myrtle trees help define the space.

room is centered on a classical parterre of common box (*Buxus sempervirens*). The shrubs form four symmetric quadrants separated by pea gravel paths, with a focal point of a large terra-cotta Italian urn planted with a golden red 'Crimson Queen' Japanese maple (*Acer palmatum*) and an overflowing skirt of fragrant clove-scented perennial Sweet William (*Dianthus barbatus*). East of the boxwood, a long brick pond was installed, marked by sentries on each corner of towering Washingtonian palms, which are surrounded by lush, dark green clumps of liriope giant evergreen (*Liriope muscari*). Filled with the golden, gracefully arching leaves of zebra grass (*Miscanthus sinensis* 'Zebrinus'), ancient Egyptian papyrus (*Cyperus papyrus*) and tropical day-blooming water lilies such as the rich, deep purple nymphaea 'Lindsey Woods', the pond is highlighted by sprays of water cascading from each corner—a practical as well as aesthetic feature, as they help drown out noise from the bustling city just beyond the garden walls. An intimate terrace was created against the brick wall, enclosing the garden from the street. Backed by a hedge of Japanese yew (*Podocarpus macrophyl-*

lus), the terrace is delineated by four flowering crape myrtle trees (*Lagerstroemia indica*) and holds several fifty-year-old camellias (*Camellia japonicum*), one of the few remaining plants original to the garden and carefully conserved during the renovation. A privet hedge of waxy-leafed Japanese ligustrum (*Ligustrum japonica*) was planted along the south border and backed with a row of hardy ironwood trees (*Olneya tesota*) to help shade the garden during the warm South Carolina afternoons.

The second room, a clipping garden, is entered by passing through a wrought-iron garden gate set between brick pillars that support an arching overhead gas-jet lantern. The clipping garden is several steps below the formal garden, enhancing separation between the rooms as well as keeping it level with the back of the house. Centered on a bowling green of lawn, the room ends in a gurgling wall fountain flanked by two sturdy sago palms (*Cycas revoluta*). The southern border of ironwood trees and Japanese ligustrum hedge was continued from the formal garden, while more privet hedges of ligustrum on the west and east were added to help define the room. Australian tree

ferns (*Cyathea cooperi*) interspersed with fragrant pink sweetheart roses (*Rosa* 'Cecile Brunner') give form and color to the beds in front of the ironwood trees. On the north, a long and striking allée of Natchez crape myrtle (*Lagerstroemia indica* x *fauriei* 'Natchez') provides visual interest throughout the year, with cinnamon bark trunks in fall and winter and masses of brilliant white blossoms in summer. The allée also screens the house and shades cutting beds of brilliant multicolored snapdragons (*Antirrhinum majus*), hydrangea lace cap (*Hydrangea macrophylla* var. *normalis*) and snowball (*Hydrangea macrophylla*), star magnolia (*Magnolia stellata*) and four violet purple 'Catwaba' crape myrtle trees on each corner. A secret garden is tucked behind a hedge of Japanese yew at the southern end of the allée. Planted with translucent green ginger (*Zingiber officinale*), lucky four-leaved shamrock clover (*Oxalis regnellii*), soft, lacy maidenhair ferns (*Adiatum capillus-veneris*) and iris, the secret garden is centered on a Gothic stone fountain and is a perfect spot to sit undisturbed, sip a cup of tea and quietly enjoy the garden's beauty.

Passing underneath a trellis covered in tangles of sweetly fragrant Confederate jasmine (*Trachelospermum jasminoides*), a brick breezeway paved with eighteenth-century plantation bricks leads past the former servants' quarters and livery (now the kitchen, offices and indoor pool) to the rear garden. A central allée of Natchez crape myrtle lined with common box separates a planting bed of pansies and trailing stems of variegated vinca vine (*Vinca major* and *V. minor* 'Variegata') from the house. A small boxwood hedge at the rear encloses tulip poplar (*Liriodendron tulipifera*, a favorite with hummingbirds), Japanese maple, white calla lilies (*Zantedeschia aethiopica*) and lace cap hydrangea. Brilliant robin's-egg-blue plumbagos are planted between the French doors of the pool house for colorful summer accents, and two annual beds are anchored with fragrant Charleston tea olive (*Osmanthus fragrans*), which smell like deliciously ripe apricots or peaches. A large, graciously spreading southern magnolia more than two hundred years old at the back helps conceal a mechanical building. Loquat trees, azaleas, oak leaf hydrangeas (*Hydrangea quercifolia*), fall and winter flowering pink *Camellia sasanqua* and elegant Savannah hollies (*Ilex* x *attenuata* 'Savannah') are planted along the driveway for privacy at the rear of the garden.

Formal, inviting and visually pleasing, this garden reflects the best of the classic elegance of historic Charleston. 🌿

ABOVE: Fragrant Sweet William overflows from the terra-cotta urn in the center of the boxwood parterre.
FACING: The formal garden leads into the second garden room, the clipping garden, which is centered on a bowling green lawn. Australian tree ferns give structure to the southern planting bed.

LEFT: A brick and wrought-iron archway leads from the formal garden into the clipping garden. FACING, TOP: A gas lantern (a favorite Charleston feature) romantically lights the archway. FACING, BOTTOM: The western end of the clipping garden is centered on a stone fountain backed by a hedge of ligustrum and bordered by a pair of sago palms.

LEFT: A Gothic sunroom encloses the clipping garden and a secret garden room hidden inside a hedge of thick Japanese yew.
ABOVE: The secret garden is centered on a Gothic stone fountain and enclosed by a tight hedge of Japanese yew.
FACING: Colorful beds of snapdragons border the house in the clipping garden.

LEFT: A long allée of Natchez crape myrtle lined with common box leads down a pea gravel path through the rear garden.
ABOVE: Delicate Egyptian papyrus is caught in the soft southern twilight.

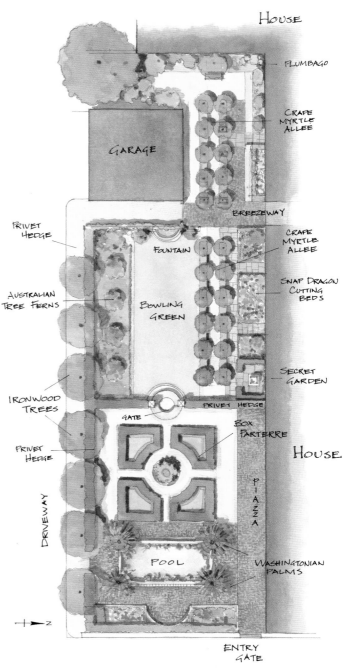

HOUSE

FLUMBAGO

CRAPE MYRTLE ALLEE

GARAGE

BREEZEWAY

PRIVET HEDGE

FOUNTAIN

CRAPE MYRTLE ALLEE

SNAP DRAGON CUTTING BEDS

AUSTRALIAN TREE FERNS

BOWLING GREEN

SECRET GARDEN

IRONWOOD TREES

PRIVET HEDGE

GATE

BOX PARTERRE

HOUSE

PRIVET HEDGE

PIAZZA

DRIVEWAY

POOL

WASHINGTONIAN PALMS

N

ENTRY GATE

TOP: Antique eighteenth-century bricks were used for the breezeway and patio connecting the clipping garden and rear garden.
BOTTOM: Beds are bordered with moss-covered bricks and mulched with pine needles.
RIGHT: Classic elegance garden plan.

JAPANESE GARDEN
IN SAN MATEO

When Joan and Achille Paladini first looked at the Japanese garden and teahouse for sale in the San Francisco suburb of San Mateo in 1988, it was a sorrowful sight to behold. The entire garden was overgrown with ivy and ferns, and the paths were not even passable. Specimen plants were dead or missing, and the large central pond had dwindled down to a muddy puddle without fish. The waterfalls had been allowed to decay (previous owners discretely ran a garden hose over the rocks when they had visitors). Even the original bamboo fence had fallen down, and the property was open to the street.

But the Paladinis were nonetheless fascinated. Mrs. Paladini, a keen gardener, went to the library and researched the garden's history. Designed by the famous Japanese gardener Makota Hagiwara (who also designed the Japanese Tea Gardens in Golden Gate Park), it had been completed in 1897 for local businessman and Japanese enthusiast Henry Pike Bowie. Later owned by Eugene De Sabla (the first developer of hydroelectric power in the area and founder of PG&E), the one-acre garden became part of his large El Cerrito estate and was the site of many celebrated social events in the early twentieth century. Untended for several years during World War II (the Japanese gardeners had all been sent to internment camps), the garden was bought and restored by a retired air force major after the war; he also enlarged the one-room teahouse into a sym-

pathetic bungalow. And somehow the estate survived, a small oasis in a surrounding subdivision of homes in the busy metropolitan Bay Area.

Mr. and Mrs. P., as they like to be called, bought this garden—formerly called Higurashi-en or "A Garden Worthy of A Day's Contemplation"—and began the laborious process of bringing it back to life. The first order of business was much-needed structural repairs. Underground piping was

FACING: Japanese gardens carefully combine vistas, or "borrowed views," to show the interplay of natural and manmade scenery. Here a traditional arched wooden bridge leads across the lake to Turtle Island. Carefully trained and pruned evergreens include (left to right) Japanese black pine (*Pinus thunbergiana*) and several varieties of Hinoki cypress (*Chamaecyparis obtusa* 'Nana Aurea' and others).

placed underneath the cement pond and connected with three large biological filters at the back of the property to keep the nearly 100,000-gallon pond clear. A two-horsepower submersible pump was installed to run the two waterfalls and also recycle water to the filters. The patio next to the original teahouse was enlarged and resurfaced with tricolor flagstones. And the bamboo fence was rebuilt after the original design to enclose the property and keep it safe from neighborhood children. Nighttime lighting was also added. Mrs. P. researched what had originally been planted and replaced hundreds of plants from specimen cherry trees such as a Weeping Higan Cherry (*Prunus subhirtella* 'Pendula') to simple Hen and chickens (*Echeveria elegans*).

The house needed extensive remodeling and updating as well. The original teahouse was suffering from serious dry rot, and its redwood siding had to be replaced. The remainder of the house also required significant work: wiring was replaced and a new kitchen, bathrooms and hardwood floors were sensitively added, all in keeping with an Eastern aesthetic.

LEFT: Ancient, carefully chosen stones and 1,000-year-old lava were used in the construction of the waterfall.
FACING, TOP: A meticulously pruned golden English yew (*Taxus baccata* 'Aurea') shelters a hardy orange (*Ponciris trifoliata* 'Flying Dragon') on a hillside above the lake. The stone lantern is a Yukimi, or "snow-viewing," variety considered at its greatest beauty when snow accumulates on its top.
FACING, BOTTOM: Silvery blue succulent Hen and chickens (*Echeveria elegans*) form a small border near the lake and are believed to keep away evil spirits.

While Mrs. P. loves working in the garden daily, she admitted to needing some help. Fortunately, one of the longtime gardeners, Tak Obata, came with the garden when the Paladinis bought it, and he continues to meticulously prune and tend to the plants today after more than forty years (he's now in his eighties), continuing a family tradition passed down to him from his father, who worked there as well. Additional gardeners also come each week to care for the pond and filters and do the heavier work.

The purpose of a Japanese tea garden is to allow its occupants to enter a state of purification and empty their minds of distractions before the tea ceremony. Everything is carefully thought out, symbolic of man's relationship with nature. Entering through the original bamboo front gates, one is transported into an enclosed world like "a drop of dew on a blade of grass" leading towards enlightenment. A path of stepping stones winds to the main garden, each stone methodically placed with respect to its shape, size, composition and color to create a juxtaposition of both natural and artificial textures, emphasizing how man-made elements are placed within a natural setting. The original teahouse, now the home's dining room, overlooks the garden. A Sen no Rikyū–style *chashitsu* (teahouse), it was built entirely of redwood without any nails and with a shoji screen that was to be closed during the tea ceremony so guests would not be distracted by the lovely views.

A large lagoon forms the heart of the garden with a picturesque miniature island—Turtle Island—in its center. Reached by a traditional arched, red wooden bridge, it is planted with carefully pruned evergreens, such as *Cotoneaster microphylla* 'Thymifolia'. A pair of life-size bronze cranes perch on the island, looking out over the water while scores of koi—some several decades old—swim in colorful schools just beneath the surface. To fully appreciate the garden, it is important to contemplate its symbolism: the koi stand for fertility, the cranes fidelity, and the turtles for long life. *Shakkei,* or using nature as a backdrop for "borrowed views," is another of the garden's central themes. Thus a stone bridge on the other side of Turtle Island leads to the far side of the garden, which is centered on a cascading waterfall made from 1,000-year-old lava from Japan. Framed by the icy blue pendant needles of a Weeping Blue Atlas cedar (*Cedrus atlantica* 'Glauca Pendula'), the waterfall's soothing sound (meant to suggest meditation) does indeed transport the visitor to a serene and calm state of mind. A large granite Kotoji lantern at the edge of the lake has two feet in the lake and two feet on the path, reflecting the interdependence of water and land.

Winding paths of stone and gravel lead around the perimeter of the lake and to other rooms in the garden. A 400-year-old hand-carved Japanese stone bridge on the north side of the lake is embellished with Kanji engravings translating as "the

bridge to eternal tranquility." A picturesque stone lantern, bought from the 1915 World's Fair in San Francisco, rests on a small hillside above. One of the rarest plants in the garden, a 200-year-old five-needle Japanese white pine (*Pinus parviflora*) was just a small bonsai in a pot when given as a gift from the emperor of Japan; now it spreads to nearly five feet. A formal garden with specimen plants, a small hillside with a bench for viewing and a Zen garden bordered with giant bamboo are some of the other sections tucked within the sanctuary.

Humans are not the only ones to appreciate the garden. Wildlife in abundance visit daily: giant blue herons, egrets and kingfishers all looking for lunch in the lake, as well as mallard ducks, squirrels and raccoons out for a stroll.

The Paladinis have made the garden their life's passion and had it placed on the National Register of Historic Places in 1993. The garden is listed by the Smithsonian Institution as the "most authentic privately owned Japanese garden" in the United States. 🌿

FACING: A Weeping Blue Atlas cedar has been methodically trained with bamboo poles across the waterfall. A purple-red Japanese maple (*Acer palmatum* 'Burgundy Lace') adds a delicate dash of color.
ABOVE, LEFT: A Japanese stone lantern bought from the 1915 San Francisco World's Fair still graces the garden.
ABOVE, RIGHT: A mediator gong was used in ancient temples to announce morning Zen; it is also good for calling guests for barbeques, the Paladinis admit.

FACING: The original teahouse has been methodically restored and preserved, including its redwood beams and shoji screens. It now is the dining room.
ABOVE: The teahouse emits a warm and magical glow at dusk; the vista is an important element of the garden's design.

FACING: The original front gates and bamboo fence were restored and enclose the entire property.

ABOVE, LEFT: Visitors to the main house, which was added to the teahouse in the 1940s, are greeted by an appropriately Oriental front door.

ABOVE, RIGHT: An Oribe stone lantern supported on a pedestal accents the hillside above the lake.

ABOVE: Dahlias add a dash of color against the ancient stone "Bridge to Eternal Tranquility" across the north end of the lake. The waterfall and hill across the lake were built from 1,000-year-old lava imported from Japan.

LEFT: Detail of the carved stone bridge with a rare, two-centuries-old five-needle Japanese white pine in the foreground.

FACING: Japanese garden plan.

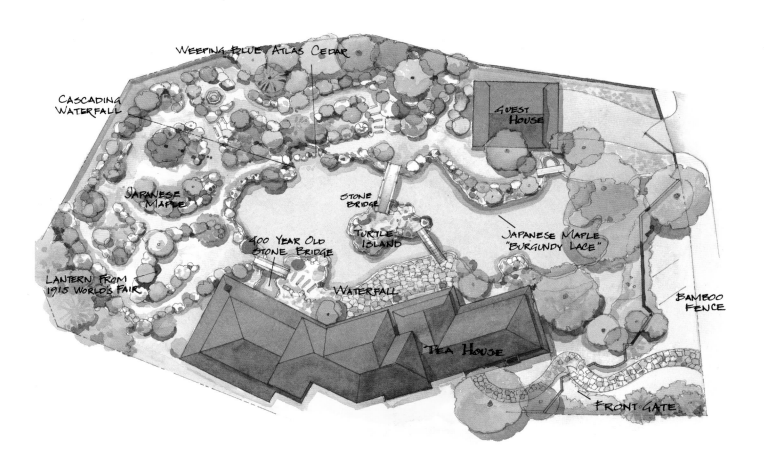

WEEPING BLUE ATLAS CEDAR

CASCADING
WATERFALL

GUEST
HOUSE

JAPANESE
MAPLE

STONE
BRIDGE

TURTLE
ISLAND

JAPANESE MAPLE
"BURGUNDY LACE"

400 YEAR OLD
STONE BRIDGE

LANTERN FROM
1915 WORLD'S FAIR

WATERFALL

BAMBOO
FENCE

TEA HOUSE

FRONT GATE

CURB APPEAL
IN SEATTLE

"Curb appeal" is a phrase that's often used to describe an alluring home, one that grabs your attention as you walk by. It can be nearly any style or design, but with something that makes people stop for a second look. Perhaps it's a storybook cottage straight out of Hansel and Gretel with swooping rooflines and a fairy-tale turret. Or maybe it's a "painted lady," a Victorian with colorfully painted gingerbread details. And sometimes it's the garden that causes cars to slow down and their drivers to point. With this house in Seattle, it's been a little of all three.

The house is an early 1900s Craftsman that was given a facelift and transformed into a high-style Victorian grande dame. Over the past two decades, the owners have added a turret, had sunflowers and griffins carved on the upper gables, and even installed roof cresting created from a cemetery fence. The house was painted in a late-nineteenth-century fall palette of deep green, burgundy, black, copper and gold. Notes in the mailbox and requests for tours quickly became commonplace, and one day the owners came home to find a wedding party posing on the front steps. People often ask, "What has been the inspiration?" Surprisingly enough, the answer is that it all began with the garden.

When the owners first bought the house two decades ago, it was covered in white vinyl siding and the yard consisted of dead grass and beds littered with broken bottles. The sole survivor of the previous landscaping

efforts was a surprisingly virulent holly plant that covered the front yard in perpetual shade. The priorities were clear: white vinyl siding would be tolerable much longer than an unattractive landscape. So, with the help of landscape designers Withey Price Landscaping, work on the yard began immediately.

As the front yard is shallow, only twenty-two feet deep, and easily overwhelmed by the two-story house, white birch trees (*Betula jacquemontii*) were planted in the parking strip to anchor the garden and visually pull it down and out towards the curb. After several years the birches became too large and were replaced by variegated English holly trees (*Ilex aquifolium*), which

FACING: The front garden is anchored by two conical hollies, large balls of boxwood and a dwarf boxwood hedge. Plants were chosen to complement the eclectic Victorian house.

ABOVE: The front slopes are planted in a lush array of sun-tolerant coleus, fuchsia, canna 'Tropicanna', pelargonium and castor bean.

LEFT: Tight shot of dahlia 'Moonfire'.

FACING, LEFT: Vintage edging tiles in the front slope set off sun-tolerant coleus, castor bean, dahlia 'Moonfire' and canna 'Bengal Tiger'.

FACING, RIGHT: Swathes of scarlet red coleus, knotweed *Persicaria microcephala* 'Red Dragon' and pelargonium 'Vancouver Centennial' are highlighted against the cool green boxwood balls in the front slopes.

have been patiently pruned into conical accents demarcating the garden's entrance.

Seattle was built on a series of hills, and many of its homes have front yard slopes for planting, although often they have been replaced with low-maintenance rock gardens and walls. The owners decided to keep the shallow front slopes intact as planting beds for color and visual interest. The owners and their landscape designers evolved a scheme of admittedly high-maintenance seasonal plantings whose colors would coordinate well with the palette of the house. While the fall and spring are attractive with winter pansies and a few bulbs, the yard really comes into its prime in the summer when it is planted out in vibrant swathes of color—hybrid, sun-tolerant cultivars of coleus in a rainbow of burgundy, chartreuse, copper and gold; dark-leafed dahlias (*Dahlia* 'Moonfire') with their bronze leaves and vibrant pale ochre and orange flowers; fancy-leafed pelargoniums such as 'Vancouver Centennial', with its intense, two-toned foliage of deep terra-cotta and chartreuse; lime green and yellow; variegated *Plectranthus*; fuchsia 'Gartenmeister Bonstedt', with reddish bronze foliage and intense, deep red single flowers that bloom all summer; and purple-foliaged castor bean (*Ricinus communis* 'Carmencita'). A favorite is the Persian Shield plant (*Strobilanthes dyerianus*) with its metallic-looking silver and purple leaves. Antique iron fencing was found to run along the top of the slopes and backed with a neatly clipped dwarf boxwood hedge (*Buxus sempervirens* 'Suffruticosa').

LEFT: A shade window box on the front porch overflows with a maidenhair fern (*Adiantum*), dracaena 'Limelight' and a multicolored bromeliad.
RIGHT, TOP: An antique iron gate was placed across the driveway.
RIGHT, BOTTOM: A discarded window grille was turned into a gate for the front steps.
FACING: The house beckons at dusk as its lights glow with rich colors echoed in the garden.

Of course, pots were needed for the front steps; so tall "Long Tom" Victorian-style pots were thrown in combinations of black and red to match the colors of the house. They were filled with fragrant lavender heliotrope (*Heliotropium arborescens*), fancy-leaved pelargoniums such as 'Mrs. Pollock', 'Skies of Italy', and 'Mrs. Henry Cox', and modern, colorful coleus cultivars such as 'Carrot Top', 'Sedona' and 'Inky Fingers'. As if there weren't already enough visual interest, more was added: a hand-carved window box with alligators and an anxious baby was designed for underneath the front window and planted with multicolored canna, orange-flowered abutilon and the tender, trailing fuchsia 'Autumnale,' which is remarkable for its kaleidoscopic deep terra-cotta pink foliage that turns yellow and then pale green through the season. Purple petunia ('Wave' series) is a favorite for the window box, and trailing variegated ivies (*Hedera* spp.) are used to soften the intense colors. To add to the mood of a Victorian garden, vintage iron griffins were added to the bottom of the porch steps, and a cast-iron Fiske fountain was also installed in the front yard.

The narrow side yard on the north, which never sees direct sun, was planted with low-maintenance hosta 'Halcyon' and 'Regal Splendor', both relatively bug-proof. Different evergreen and herbaceous ferns, mostly forms of *Dryopteris*, along with the unusual tatting fern (*Athyrium felix-femina* 'Frizelliae') were used to fill in the narrow planting beds along the house, along with variegated Persian ivy (*Hedera colchica* 'Dentata Variegata') in creamy white and slate green.

An arched lattice fence topped with an arbor was built to enclose the tiny back-yard, and table grapes 'Interlaken' and 'Niagara' were planted to clamber over it. Another variegated Persian ivy (*Hedera colchica* 'Sulphur Heart') was trained up the lattice arches. Two twelve-foot-tall locust trees (*Robinia pseudoacacia* 'Frisia') were found and, along with a red-leafed Japanese maple (*Acer palmatum*), used to screen the backyard from neighboring houses, which look down directly into the small space. After several years of effort, the owners gave up keeping a lawn alive in the backyard shade and replaced it with a more practical ellipse of colored gravel edged with antique clay edging tiles. More Victorian garden ornaments were found: a pair of large terra-cotta balls; a set of wrought-iron benches and a match-ing chair; and a massive, late-nineteenth-century, five-foot-tall iron planter of a stag's head supporting an open-weave basket—a typically curious Victorian creation.

The owners admit they never stopped to consider that they were creating some-thing that would attract attention but soon learned that if you make it, they will come. The garden and house have been featured in newspapers, magazines and on HGTV and are even pictured on the observation deck of Seattle's Space Needle as a representation of the local neighborhood. Want to create something special? Follow your muse, the owners advise, but remember you will have to deal with the attention it may bring.

FACING: A whimsical Victorian fountain splashes in the front yard.
TOP: Fuchsia 'Autumnale' dangles in front of the colorfully carved alligator on the front window box.
BOTTOM: A nineteenth-century cast-iron griffin guards the front steps.

ABOVE: Fragrant purple *Heliotropium arborescens* is mixed with burgundy coleus in a pot.
LEFT: Assorted coleus in the front slopes.
FACING: Fuchsias 'Firecracker' and 'Gartenmeister Bonstedt' and coleus 'Sedona' fill the pots on the front steps.

ABOVE: Surrounded by an arched lattice fence, the backyard is a serene shade garden.
FACING, TOP LEFT: Vintage English edging tiles line an ellipse of colored gravel in the backyard.
FACING, TOP RIGHT: Spiky *Iris foetidissima* 'Variegata', white-stemmed bramble (*Rubus cockburnianus*) and spotted laurel (*Aucuba japonica*) provide a pleasing backdrop for terra-cotta balls and a garden chair.
FACING, BOTTOM LEFT: Detail of a cast-iron stag head planter.
FACING, BOTTOM RIGHT: A wrought-iron Victorian garden seat is nestled against the ferns in the backyard.

LEFT: An arched lattice gate entices viewers into the small private backyard.
ABOVE: A stained-glass arch demarcates the entrance to the backyard on the north side of the house.
FACING: Curb appeal garden plan.

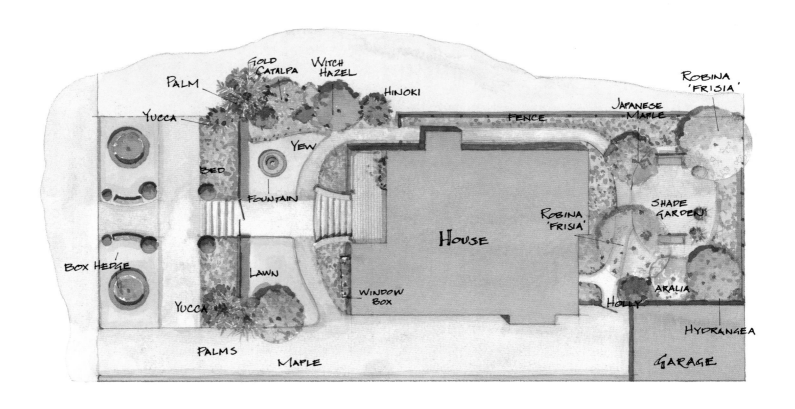

Labels within the illustration:

PALM

GOLD CATALPA

WITCH HAZEL

HINOKI

YUCCA

YEW

BED

FOUNTAIN

ROBINA 'FRISIA'

JAPANESE MAPLE

FENCE

SHADE GARDEN

ROBINA 'FRISIA'

BOX HEDGE

LAWN

YUCCA

WINDOW BOX

HOUSE

ARALIA

HOLLY

HYDRANGEA

PALMS

MAPLE

GARAGE

VICTORIAN GRANDEUR
IN CHARLESTON

The Calhoun Mansion in Charleston is one of the largest and most spectacular homes in a city of many beautiful historic residences. Built in 1876 near the Charleston Harbor, the 24,000-square-foot Italianate villa was Charleston's most opulent home of the time. Designed for wealthy banker William P. Russell, it is named for its second resident, William's son-in-law Patrick Calhoun. The mansion has fortunately always remained a single-family residence, and in 1998, its owners commissioned well-known Charleston landscape architect Sheila Wertimer to bring its gardens forward into the twentieth century in a sympathetic manner reflective of the architecture and history of the house.

Sheila took the formality of an English estate as her inspiration and replaced the existing lawns with a classic series of brick parterres, wrapping them around the house to give the landscape an elegant, traditional appeal.

The grounds are divided into a series of rooms, each centered on a sculpture or water feature and connected by meandering brick paths. The front garden, entered through substantial wrought-iron gates, sets the mood with a hedge of tightly clipped Japanese boxwood (*Buxus microphylla*) backed by a higher screen of lustrous, dark green Japanese yew (*Podocarpus macrophyllus*). Together they act as foundation plantings against the front portico. The delicate leaves of Japanese maple (*Acer palmatum*) spread over each side of the front gates and shade curving beds of thick 'Nana' dwarf mondo grass (*Ophiopogon japonicus*). Large triangles of pure white azaleas (*Azalea indica* 'G.G. Gerbing') on either side of the entrance are backed by Japanese boxwood hedges, which nestle against the wrought-iron fence and help screen the garden from the street. A brick path leads north to a circle outlined in spokes of tightly clipped Japanese boxwood, which in turn enclose large, luminous orbs of dwarf yaupon holly (*Ilex vomitoria* 'Shadows'). Clustered like giant bubbles rising from a hidden underground

FACING: An antique lead statue of Mercury presides over a cluster of large orbs of dwarf yaupon holly set between the spokes of a circle of Japanese boxwood in the front garden.

LEFT: The grand front portico is accented with foundation plantings of tightly clipped Japanese boxwood backed by a higher screen of Japanese yew.

ABOVE: A sturdy wrought-iron Victorian fence encloses the gardens of the Calhoun Mansion.

FACING: An antique statue of Mercury is silhouetted against the gas lanterns illuminating the front entrance to the Calhoun Mansion at twilight.

spring, the orbs of yaupon holly are presided over by a tall lead statue of the winged messenger Mercury holding his caduceus aloft to the heavens.

The north garden, a brick-paved parterre, is designed as a water garden to be appreciated above from the wide piazzas running the length of the house. Two circular koi ponds planted with multicolored Louisiana iris flank a central pool that is highlighted by spraying jets of water on each corner. Classical symmetry is reinforced by towering Italian cypress (*Cupressus sempervirens*) on each corner of the parterre, along with a pair of olive green sago palms (*Cycas revoluta*) in cast-iron planters next to the house. Hedges of Japanese boxwood backed by Japanese yew are continued down the north border to separate the garden from the driveway.

The north garden leads to the rear garden on the eastern end of the property. Another circle of Japanese boxwood is punctuated by a solitary Japanese stone lantern in its center. Beyond this, at the back of the rear garden, a three-tiered antique cast-iron fountain provides a soothing respite from city noise just beyond the garden walls. The fountain is encircled by freestanding stone columns crowned with tangles of Japanese wisteria (*Wisteria floribunda*), which are much prized for their masses of grape-scented lavender blooms each spring. Privet hedges of waxy-leafed Japanese ligustrum (*Ligustrum japonicum*) help define the room. A spreading live oak (*Quercus virginiana*) (the Southern symbol of strength) at the end of the garden provides shade from the strong afternoon sun as well as privacy from neighboring homes.

The Victorian age was one of splendor and beauty, and the nineteenth-century grandeur of the Calhoun Mansion has been aptly captured in the classic elegance of its surrounding gardens.

BOXWOOD BASICS

Boxwood (so named because when cut, the cross-section of the stem is actually square) has been a staple for gardeners for many centuries. Used for topiary and edging borders as well as massing in beds, this versatile plant has more than seventy varieties. Slow-growing English, or dwarf, boxwood is popular in smaller gardens, as it rarely grows over three feet tall, while with more room, common box can reach up to thirty feet. Hardy to zone 5, box can be grown in full sun or partial shade; Korean box is a good choice if you live in a northern climate, as it is more tolerant to winter cold. Sturdy and easy to grow, boxwood does have a few basic requirements:

1. Well-drained soil is crucial, as roots may rot if waterlogged.
2. Mulching is much appreciated by the box's shallow root system, but be sure to limit the mulch to one inch and keep it six inches from the stems to avoid damage by mice or voles. Carefully weed by hand around the base to minimize soil and root disturbance.
3. Thinning late each winter is important to promote light and air circulation inside the boxwood and to encourage new growth within the canopy.
4. Cleaning the inside of the plant with a strong hose spray during the summer is also an excellent way to clean debris inside the plant and improve airflow.

While fairly drought tolerant, box does best with regular deep soakings with a soaker hose, especially when newly transplanted.

FACING: A winding brick path bordered by hedges of clipped Japanese boxwood leads across the front garden. A pair of sago palms in antique cast-iron planters add a note of elegance. RIGHT: The setting sun glistens off the globes of dwarf yaupon holly in the front garden.

A trio of pools in the north garden seen from above, on the second-floor piazza.
Symmetry and balance are used to define the elegance of the brick parterre.

The brick path continues around the house to the north garden, which is centered on pools set in a brick parterre. Tall Italian cypress stand as sentries on each corner.

Delicate lavender-and-white Louisiana irises grow in one of the koi ponds.

ABOVE, LEFT: Another circle of Japanese boxwood is punctuated with a Japanese stone lantern in the north garden. The rear garden lies just beyond.

ABOVE, CENTER: A three-tiered antique cast-iron fountain provides a pleasant focus in the rear garden.

ABOVE, RIGHT: An antique lead swan merrily spouts water over one of the koi ponds.

FACING: The rear garden, seen from the third-floor piazza, shows the fountain with brick paths coming off the central axis. Japanese wisteria climbs over stone columns, marking the entrance of each path.

ABOVE: An antique lead eagle perches on the rim of the cast-iron fountain, which centers the rear garden.

RIGHT, TOP: A fanciful Victorian stone birdhouse perches on a stone branch in the rear garden.

RIGHT, BOTTOM: An enchanting Pan plays his pipes in a small clearing in the south garden, which is composed of large azaleas and evergreen shrubbery.

FACING: Victorian grandeur garden plan.

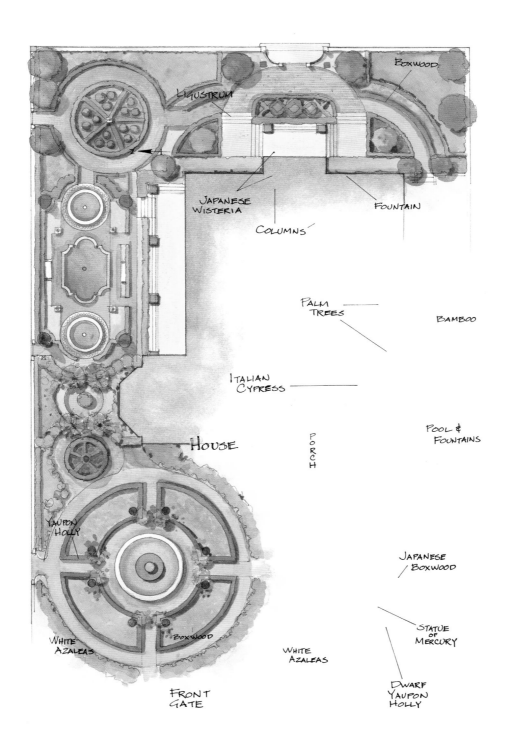

BOXWOOD

LIGUSTRUM

JAPANESE
WISTERIA

COLUMNS

FOUNTAIN

PALM
TREES

BAMBOO

ITALIAN
CYPRESS

POOL &
FOUNTAINS

P
O
R
C
H

HOUSE

JAPANESE
/ BOXWOOD

YAUPON
HOLLY

STATUE
OF
MERCURY

WHITE
AZALEAS

BOXWOOD

WHITE
AZALEAS

DWARF
YAUPON
HOLLY

FRONT
GATE

FAR EASTERN MYSTIQUE
IN PORTLAND

While Portland, Oregon, is known for its rainy climate and verdant landscapes, one usually doesn't expect to find there a garden of serene stone Buddhas, sandstone fragments from ancient Indian temples and softly tinkling wind chimes. But then, Jeffrey Bale is not your typical gardener. Born in Eugene, with a degree in landscape architecture from the University of Oregon, Jeffrey admits that his first job after college at a Portland horticultural firm lasted about twenty minutes. He immediately realized he was not suited for the corporate world and so began his own garden maintenance and design business. Using his small 30-by-33-foot-deep Portland garden for practice, he patiently perfected the arts of plant culture, masonry and soil culture.

In order to escape the dreary Oregon winters, Jeffrey began a now several-decades-old tradition of traveling December through April to warmer and more exotic climes—the Far and Near East, Asia, Central and South America. Each voyage taught him something new. He spent over two weeks, for example, at the Taj Majal, sketching and studying its gardens and architecture. Back home in Portland, his garden evolved into a translation of his travels—his own version of an Eastern paradise, a place of serenity and sensuous beauty.

The property was not in the best of neighborhoods—the house next door belonged to drug dealers and was eventually seized and boarded up by the police; thus landscape screening from the neighbors became a

priority. Jeffrey built seat-height mortared stone walls across the front yard. He planted for privacy, including a now 22-foot-tall, two-decades-old vine maple (*Acer circinatum*) whose delicate branches effectively screen the garden from the sidewalk. Also sharing guard duty are a native cascara tree (*Rhamnus purshiana*) that is quite popular with the birds and an ancient, bushy camellia with peppermint-candy-striped blossoms that was original to the house. A climbing hydrangea (*Hydrangea anomala* subsp. *petiolaris*) was allowed to clamber over the front of the house to cover up a much-needed paint job

FACING:
A wall of architectural sandstone fragments from India anchors the east end of the back garden.

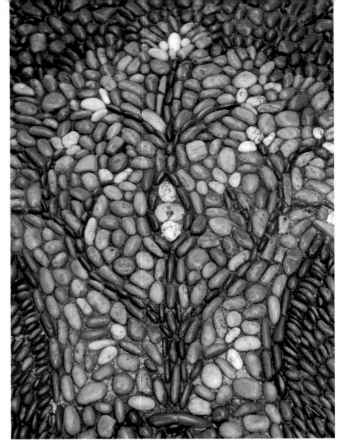

and help make the house blend into the garden and disappear. A mahonia 'Arthur Menzies', with its spectacular December display of yellow buds on long stems much like delicate, glowing pearls on a string, was planted by the front door, while another mahonia ('Charity', or lily of the valley, bush) was added in the back, its cheery yellow blooms providing a joyful display from November through March. Rhododendrons do well in the cool, moist climate of the Pacific Northwest, and a large, hardy rhododendron 'Cunningham's White' was added to the front. Due to Jeffrey's religious and patient deadheading, it rewards him each May with a spectacular display of sparkling white blossoms.

Seven years ago Jeffrey purchased the neighboring house (by then condemned), and began the laborious process of its remodel. Travels to Spain and exposure to the extraordinary Park Guell, a fantasy of mosaic structures built by Antoni Gaudi between 1900 and 1914 on a rocky hillside in Barcelona, inspired Jeffrey to begin working with mosaics. After removing piles of garbage from the house's front yard, he laid down his own hand-designed pebble mosaic pathways, incorporating symbols of protection—a pair of eyes, an endless knot, a Western rattlesnake. In the northeast corner he carved out a small prayer niche with an intricate pebble mosaic prayer rug leading to a heavenly sandstone Buddha he had purchased in India. The niche was enclosed with the gargantuan *Canna* 'Musifolia' (banana canna), which grows up to twelve feet tall, for a tall and narrow summer screen; trailing flowering maple (*Abutilon megapotamicum*) was allowed to wind around it. Golden Japanese forest grass (*Hakonechloa macra* 'Aureola') and compact, creamy yellow *Corokia* x *virgata* ('Sunsplash') provide summer color, while across the back, a grove of golden bamboo (*Phylostachys aurea*) helps complete the canopy, making it a private, enchanting altar and retreat.

The two small backyards were merged into one and the central axis paved with three-fourths-inch-round rock to tie the two rooms together. In order to screen an unsightly house next door (only a few feet from the property line), Jeffrey built a wall along the southeast border for a raised planting bed using stones from around the world, many from his South American forays. Against the eastern edge of the yard, he raised an eye-catching wall of sandstone architectural carvings, fragments of demolished buildings he collected from the city of Jodhpur in Rajasthan, India. Built in the style of a Persian shrine, the wall is composed of niches, framed in scalloped arches and backed with mosaic stones and tiles, overlooking a small reflecting pool. Bronze Buddhas and Hindu deities from Thailand oversee the garden from the niches above.

Jeffrey made his own interpretation of a harem divan for enjoying his Eastern retreat by installing a plywood platform over the top of a discarded claw-foot tub and layering it with brightly colored cushions and throws. Lying on the converted divan and sipping spiced tea from the samovar on a warm summer evening, one is easily transported to Bali or Bombay. Oriental carpets laid over the gravel during warm, dry weather add to the feel of a lush tropical paradise.

Colorful plants were chosen for the back gardens. The pure white leaves of a rambunctious kiwi (*Actinidia kolomikta*) make a stunning backdrop for a passionate purple lilac; both bloom in late May. A delicate pink-flowered Japanese wisteria (*Wisteria floribunda*) begins to bloom as the kiwi's leaves turn pink in June, and its intoxicating scent wafts indoors through the kitchen windows. Twice-bearing raspberries are one of Jeffrey's favorites, and brambles are allowed to spread throughout the garden, their red fruits hanging like

FACING, LEFT: A smiling Buddha sits on an altar in a small niche created in the front garden. Hand-laid stone mosaics mimic an Oriental prayer rug. Golden bamboo forms a privacy screen across the back.
FACING, RIGHT: Sensual rock design.
RIGHT, TOP: A hand-laid stone mosaic path in the form of a rattlesnake slithers across the front yard.
RIGHT, BOTTOM: Stones in the front steps add to the organic charm of the garden.

precious ruby pendants and lasting from midsummer until November.

An Italian honey fig tree ('Lattarula') was planted behind the former drug house for shade and privacy, and it now bears a bumper crop of sweet green-skinned fruit with honey-colored flesh that Jeffrey enjoys picking from his bedroom window and eating in bed. An evergreen michelia (*Michelia maudiae*), its leathery green leaves covered with fragrant white blossoms each spring, and a narrow hedge of ebony black bamboo (*Phyllostachys nigra* 'Bory') planted within a rhizome barrier were added along the southern border to further screen out the neighbors. A vigorous eighteen-foot-tall hardy banana (*Musa basjoo*) (which can grow two feet a week in the summer) arches out over the center of the back garden each summer, and occasionally its blooms produce small clumps of quite inedible bananas.

Containers are used for summer color and hold richly hued coleus (*Solenostemon scutellarioides*): chartreuse with black purple veining 'Gay's Delight', glowing orange 'Sedona', and bright purple and iridescent magenta 'Stained Glass' among the favorites. Fuchsia 'Gartenmeister Bohnstedt'—good for attracting hummingbirds—and the variegated leaves and large apricot bells of flowering maple (*Abutilon megapotamicum*) 'Souvenir du Bonn' are also used for more visual interest and display.

Exotic, personal, and refreshingly unique, this garden shows how travel can indeed lend a new perspective, inspiring beauty and sensuality in the best of landscape design.

LEFT, TOP: Niches of sandstone carvings from Indian temples in the back garden wall hold benevolently smiling Buddhas.
LEFT, BOTTOM: A marble Buddha looks out over the fountain in the back garden wall. Note the use of pebble and rock mosaics.
FACING: The back garden wall of Buddhas fronts a small reflecting pool, whose gurgling fountain helps drown out neighborhood noises.

FACING: The house is painted in colors of the tropics—bright yellows, blues and reds. Containers are used for annual color accents.
ABOVE: An Oriental copper bell hanging from a bamboo trellis enhances the sensual experience.
RIGHT, TOP: Brightly colored dahlias float in a stone basin for a touch of color.
RIGHT: An assortment of stones and ceramic fragments await placement.

FACING, LEFT: A stone head of a Buddha is enclosed in a sandstone architectural fragment.
FACING, RIGHT: In the side yard, a diminutive stone Buddha prays among piles of stones collected on travels.
LEFT: A sandstone Buddha wears a necklace of dried nasturtiums in a small prayer niche in the front garden.
ABOVE: A stone Buddha is tucked in a private corner of the back garden as a piece of sculpture.

TOP: Turkish pillows and throws are scattered across the back garden divan, actually just an old bathtub covered with plywood. Oriental carpets laid across the stone paths in dry weather lend an opulent touch.
BOTTOM, LEFT: Turkish lanterns light the garden at night, providing an exotic and alluring glow.
BOTTOM, RIGHT: The hand-built stone retaining wall in the back garden was created for raised planting beds.
FACING: Far Eastern mystique garden plan.

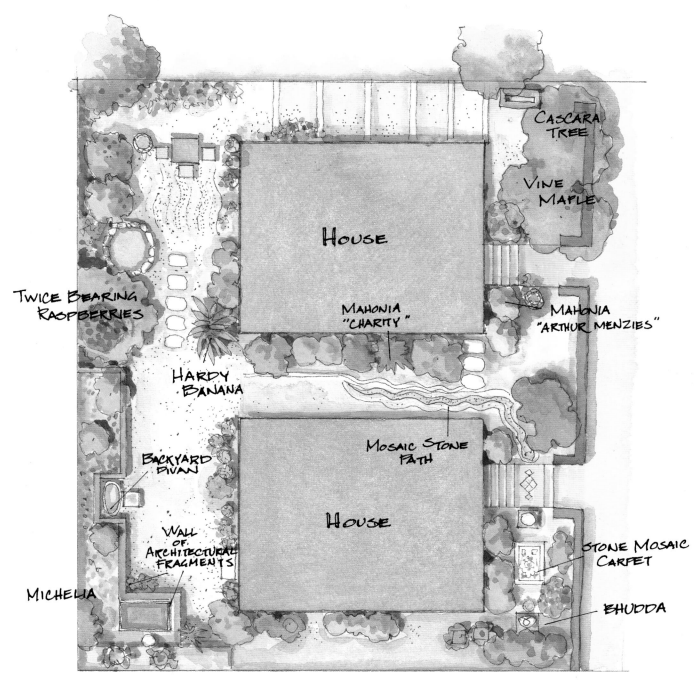

CASCARA TREE

VINE MAPLE

TWICE BEARING RASPBERRIES

HOUSE

MAHONIA "CHARITY"

MAHONIA "ARTHUR MENZIES"

HARDY BANANA

BACKYARD DIVAN

MOSAIC STONE PATH

WALL OF ARCHITECTURAL FRAGMENTS

HOUSE

STONE MOSAIC CARPET

MICHELIA

BHUDDA

GOLDEN BAMBOO